The Art of Waiting on God

A gathering of God's Remnant into a place

of readiness and active service

By

Delilah Spivey

Table of Contents

Dedication

I had no plans to include a dedication in this, my first book, but one day, I sat down to write, and God began to speak. He reminded me of my first visit to my new church home, so I dedicate this book in celebration of my pastor, Bishop Marlin J. Reid.

In 2022, God led me to leave a church that I loved dearly. I had been a member there for 30-plus years. I cried for two years after I left. I couldn't even drive by the building without tears, and there were many times when I had to remind myself that crying and driving is never a good combination. After some stumbling, I arrived at The River New Wine Glory in Livonia, Michigan. I've never been a church hopper, but if I'm coming under new leadership, I will observe that leader for a long time in order to make sure I am connected to excellence. It only took two months before I decided to join The River.

In April 2023, with some measure of frustration I said to God, "You cannot just let me keep running around without a pastor. Please tell me where to go!" It was that weekend that I walked into The River on the last Sunday of the month. They were celebrating the church's sixteenth anniversary, and I learned that Pastor Reid would not be preaching. I thought "Lord, if he's not preaching, how will I know if this is where I'm supposed to be?" Before turning the service over to the guest minister, he took the time to chronicle the history of how the church began. When he shared the prophetic words that had been delivered to him sixteen years prior about what The River would become, those words lodged in my heart immediately. I rushed to write them down as soon as I got home. At the end of the service, the guest speaker began ministering to people at the altar and Pastor Reid took the mic to assist him—singing his heart out, even though the worship team could have done that. And I thought "Wow, this man is real!" But something else happened. The spirit of seeing and knowing kicked in, and I heard these two things: #1 This man REALLY loves God; #2 He is a servant. (Sometime later, God said "soldier.") When I think I've heard from God, I tend to keep my mouth shut and my eyes open. Two years later, I can say with certainty that I did hear from God accurately that day, and He was so right.

Although I had received years of training in the Word of God, I quickly realized that God had sent me to The River to transform me into a servant who knows how to serve God with excellence. There are millions of Christian men and women who are heedless of the fact that they've been called into service by the Holy Spirit. They are dissatisfied with how their lives have turned out. They end up seeking to get as much out of life in this natural world as possible, but it only turns into selfishness, emptiness and greed. They go through many bright, shiny doors, but they miss the greatest door of opportunity, the fact that they have been called into The Service of The King. Called out of being hearers only. Called to be doers of the Word with signs and wonders following. It is because you stayed in the secret place of the Most High that God's anointing rests on you, Bishop Reid. When anyone carries out a life assignment in the face of great opposition and pain without quitting, they become marked with excellence. Because you've gone through the fire, I and many others have the opportunity to learn the art of waiting on God. I salute you, sir, and I know that God does, too.

CHAPTER 1
A CURRENT JOB OPENING

It was the Fall of 2021, and I was at church. The evangelist onstage began to sing words of adoration to the Lord. Her voice rang out in a soft melody of worship in the sanctuary. It was so beautiful and so skillful. So personal. It was very striking in the natural realm but also in the spirit realm. It commanded the room as she courted her Creator, and it turned everyone's attention to God, seated on His throne.

It was so beautiful, in fact, that when I got home, I listened to the recording again. And again.

And again.

When I finally let it rest, I sat there in the silence of my house not knowing what to do next. Witnessing this intimate exchange had made me begin to examine myself and the depth of my relationship with God. Then I heard the voice of the Lord speak:

"They rush to the banisters of heaven to hear her when she gets started (worshipping) because they want to see what's going to happen next."

Do you know how to give God so much loving attention that the residents of heaven itself stop what they're doing so that they can see what's going to happen next? Do you know how to create an atmosphere in the spirit realm that becomes a sweet odor that rises up to Jehovah? We have yet to understand that when we worship in spirit and in truth, something happens.

There is a job posting that has been listed for quite some time, for centuries, in fact, and it will never be taken down because it will always be current. This job posting is listed in the Bible in the book of John:

"But the hour cometh and now is when the true worshippers shall worship the Father in spirit and in truth, for the Father seeketh such to worship Him. God is a Spirit, and they that worship Him must worship Him in spirit and in truth."
(John 4:23-24)

You may wonder why God is seeking those who will worship Him. One reason is because worship is a divine communication channel that intimately binds us to Him. Does He have a recruiter who proactively contacts people, inviting them into deeper times of worship? Yes, the recruiter's name is the Holy Spirit. In the United States, when men are sent military draft notices, they receive a letter from the President of the country informing them that they are ordered to report for induction into the Armed Forces. They must report to a particular place on a particular date at a pre-determined time. There is no flexibility in this order, and failure to respond appropriately can have serious consequences such as legal action, fines or imprisonment. God, on the other hand, does not order us to show up for worship. He invites us. He even woos us to spend time with Him. Although the call to worship and to spend time with God is not forced like a draft notice, failure to do so can leave your spiritual life flat. It makes you ineffective in a lost and dying world. Worship is a place of empowerment.

The evangelist that I mentioned worshipped because she knows that worship is God's love language. She knows how to get into His presence at the drop of a hat. In this day and age, every Christian believer needs to know how to get into His presence quickly. We need to know how to function in spiritual things skillfully, with genuineness knowing who God is. This is what is meant by "in spirit and in truth." Truth is higher than facts, situations and circumstances, yet many have made popular the saying "Walk in your truth." You may have facts, situations and circumstances, but God's Word is the only truth because it has the ability to change facts, situations and circumstances.

When you worship, you enter into a greater measure of the Presence of God. And if you are a student of the Word of God, knowledge of the Word enables you to use language that affirms how great Jehovah is. We reverence and adore Him, and He responds by coming on the scene. Yes, He is omnipresent, but a deeper and stronger measure of His presence shows up, and suddenly, you know He's in the room. You know you're not alone, and He begins to share His heart with you, telling you things you would not know unless you had proactively shown up to worship. Even while working on this section of the book, my heart cries out to have a place to be alone and worship Him.

The Hebrew word for worship is avodah. This same word also translates to work and service. In the corporate world, the phrase "corporate culture" refers to the shared values, beliefs and behaviors that define how a company's employees interact and conduct business, basically outlining the "personality" of the organization. In the Church, we've created revival culture, healing culture, faith culture, prosperity culture, and religious rituals. When will the Church begin to teach service culture, encouraging mature believers to become proactive about serving God as the Spirit of God directs? This is where real effectiveness begins to happen in The Kingdom of God. Touching the world through service needs to be taught until it's firmly ingrained in the hearts and minds of every believer in Christ. Jesus was a lot of things to a lot of people in his earthly ministry, but at the end of the day, the best label we could ever give him is servant. What is the personality of today's Church? Is it religious activities, traditions, certain modes of dress, lofty titles, preacher worship, chicken dinners and powerless rituals that are repeated from one generation to another?

The art of waiting on God is service, and serving God needs to become the "personality" of the Church.

CHAPTER 2
THE VIBRATION OF THE BROKEN

About seven years ago, I had an online blog where I would break down churchy things for the unchurched. This is a group that I care about, and I heard the Spirit of the Lord tell me to write an article called The Vibration of the Broken. I knew it was His instruction, and even though I announced to my readers that this new article was coming soon, I was unable to write it. I chickened out because I knew that as soon as my unintended audience (church people) saw it, I would be censored for use of the word vibration. It sounded too New Age, it's not in the Bible, she's getting off course. I heard all the chatter before it could begin. As we examine the vibration of the broken, I must first tell you a personal fact about me. One of my favorite songs is Gangsta's Paradise, released in 1995. The artist is Coolio.

Surprising? I know, but listen to it online and then go read the lyrics. The lyrics hurt the first time I heard them while watching the movie Dangerous Minds. The lyrics still hit me like a tight-fisted punch today. So, when I use the word vibration, it means this: Vibration is the motion that results when the equilibrium of an object has been disturbed. Equilibrium is balance, stability, equality and peace.

An example of this happens when you kick one of those large tin cans that you purchase at the hardware store. It will vibrate from the kick, especially if it's empty. You might make a dent in it if you kick hard enough. It's no longer the shiny, silver can that it was when it was manufactured. Dents are synonymous with damage. Even when you see a dented can at the supermarket, you don't choose that one. You choose the one behind it because you wonder if the aluminum has seeped into the food in a greater measure, damaging the contents.

We have a generation of young people whose ability to live, grow and develop has been damaged. They've been kicked before their lives could begin, before their education could begin, and before their spiritual development could begin. Trauma has already shown up like a monster with long, skinny, powerful fingers to damage and choke the beauty of life out of them. Some come from broken homes and have no idea what it's like to have a strong father figure setting safe boundaries for them. When they reach young adulthood, they show up with a survival mentality. They do what they have to do in order to survive, to have basic needs met, to function in society and to have some type of pleasure. If you listened to the song and watched the movie Dangerous Minds, you may have a certain demographic in mind at this point, but those raised in poverty and lack are not the only ones who have been broken.

We are all familiar with the negative social situations that life presents sometimes. Whether it's conflicts, misunderstandings, or moments of isolation, these challenges are part of the human experience. Navigating them can be difficult, but they also shape our growth and resilience.

There are people who appear to function well in society, but if given a closer view, you discover surface behaviors that offend others they come into contact with. They cannot handle their finances, can't maintain a good relationship, treat employees unfairly in order to get ahead, sleep with as many people as they desire. They are loaded with debt, don't respect the sanctity of marriage, or maybe they're serial marriers or have commitment phobias. Some use alcohol as a crutch and a coping mechanism because they don't know what else to do. Their best friendships are formed with those who drink on a regular basis, and they segregate themselves from those who don't drink alcohol.

There are finger pointers because someone else is always at fault, and there are those who function better in chaos because an atmosphere of peace makes them uncomfortable. Many are in failing health—mentally, emotionally and physically. Some have a high school education, some a college degree and others are even more highly educated and appear to be quite successful. These everyday people also do what they have to do to survive, to have basic needs met, to function in society and to have some type of pleasure. Often, their methods of achieving goals and dreams lead to hurt for themselves as well as for those in their sphere of influence. They are trapped in a cycle of pain.

These, my friends, are the broken, and their behaviors are the vibrations of the broken.

God will speak to His people about the broken if they are listening. He will empower those who spend time with Him if they have a strong desire to serve Him, but most of God's children come to Him in order to get something other than an assignment from Heaven. Today's believer in Jesus, church goer, whatever you'd like to call them, has been found lacking in terms of compassion for the lost. The average church goer is satisfied that they've found salvation, but inwardly, they hope someone else will "tell the rest." It seems too daunting a job, a job they do not feel equipped for.

The Remnant

I remember being a shy teenager falling in love with God more and more each year. I recall how I would go upstairs to a window in our house, and I would make up songs, kneel down at that open window, look up at the sky and I would sing those songs to God. There was a desire in my heart, and I remember the words that formed:

I want to do something for God, something big, because He deserves it.

I wasn't looking for fame and fortune. I was too shy for that. All I knew was that God deserved the best and the most that little old me could give Him. All I had was desire. Many of you also have desire, and you've had that desire for a long time. It is still resident in your heart of hearts, buried under piles of other things, but it's there.

Every pastor knows that out of his total congregation, there is always a church within the church. People come for a myriad of reasons: tradition, an opportunity to dress up, out of duty, to hear good music, to promote their business, to get a good position in the church, to cultivate favor with the pastor, to leave the kids in the nursery for a couple of hours, to look for a potential spouse, and so on.

8

But Pastor knows there are those who have a heart for God and the things of God. They come more frequently than once a week. They can take correction. They volunteer. They clean up sheep droppings because the condition of the house of God matters. They serve in the church and are faithful in their support. They consistently give financial support. They actually have a regular prayer life. They know the Word of God and how to apply it successfully. They walk in a measure of the power of God. These are The Remnant.

The Remnant find it difficult to walk away from the stirrings in their heart. The Remnant is a small minority of people who will remain faithful to God because it's not enough that they are saved and going to heaven. It's not enough that they've learned how to get answers to prayer. It's not enough that they've experienced the healing power of God in their own bodies. It's not enough that they've been transformed from being cheaters, liars and thieves who have no peace. It's not enough that they've stopped sleeping with everything that moves. It's not enough that fear is no longer their master. They want to see others set free, too.

Are you a lifelong student of God's Word or a casual fan? Do you have knowledge of how to wait on God? Do you have an appetite to learn more about the art of waiting on God? This book is written to that Remnant, those who still have fire in their hearts and cannot take for granted all that God has done for them. They've seen God move in answer to prayer and by His spiritual gifts. It's much too late to tell them God does not exist or that He doesn't move in people's lives today. You cannot convince them that you can't hear from God because they've received answers to specific questions from Him already. It's too late! They're addicted to God. They love Him. They pursue Him. They won't turn back.

CHAPTER 3
THE SERVICE INDUSTRY

What Makes a Good Waiter?

One Spring, a prophetic person said to me, "Delilah, God loves a good waiter." That didn't sound good to me. It's not what I wanted to hear at the time. There is something that I've been believing God for and waiting on for decades, and there are zero signs that it's about to happen anytime soon.

I left our meeting slightly disappointed to say the least. However, that sentence would not leave me alone. "God loves a good waiter." I didn't push it aside in anger and resentment, but I allowed Holy Spirit to speak to my heart, and a new revelation began to form. These thoughts rose up:

> *God loves a good waiter.*
>
> *Not a selfish, preoccupied waiter.*
>
> *Not a mean waiter.*
>
> *Not an obnoxious waiter.*
>
> *Not an entitled waiter.*
>
> *Not a crying waiter.*
>
> *But a waiter who practices excellence in service.*

The Spirit of God was not talking about someone who sits around tapping their fingers on the table while waiting for God to do something. He was talking about a server. A good waiter does four primary things. He or she greets the guests and makes them feel welcome. He takes the orders. He deals with issues and special requests. He is very attentive, as if no request is too demanding or too difficult. Some of the characteristics of a good waiter can be found in these words:

Patient, positive, friendly, good communicator, observant, efficient, attentive to detail, good delivery, professional, makes sure the customer wants for nothing, leaves nothing undone. All of these things bring satisfaction to the customer, and a pleasant experience guarantees they will return again hoping to be served by the same wait staff.

If you read the Dedication of this book, you will recall the story of my first visit to The River and that the pastor of the church was not the speaker that day. I was frustrated because I wouldn't be able to know if I belonged there if I didn't hear him speak. However, the spirit of seeing and knowing kicked in, and I saw (heard on the inside) two things. The first thing was "This man really loves God." That was good. I could relate to that because the Bible clearly teaches us that if you truly love God, you will obey Him. That is the top indicator of whether you love Him or not. If your behavior permits you to do a plethora of things that are opposite of what His Word says, then that's how you know you don't care much for the Creator. You are just a casual fan. We read the acid test for true love in the Book of John.

"If ye love me, keep my commandments."
(John 14:15)

So, when the Holy Spirit said this man really loves God, I was relieved that I was not in the company of a wolf in sheep's clothing. He loves God, so he's living his life according to what the Bible instructs. But the second thing the Spirit of God said was "He is a servant." In grade school, we learned that an indentured servant was someone who agreed to work for a set number of years in exchange for passage to the New World. I thought it was nice that God pointed him out as a servant, but servanthood is more than just nice. I would go on to observe and to learn how highly God values service in The Kingdom. I would also gain a greater understanding of how God looks at those who are committed to serving Him.

The Butler

Research shows that good waiters often quit the service business for various reasons and go on to other endeavors, but there are some in the service industry who do not move on to other endeavors. They choose service as a career. Sometimes, it chooses them. If you've ever watched a good movie about serving in a wealthy household, behind the scenes reveals what waiters, butlers, house maids, valets, footmen and housekeepers experience and endure.

Top tier service staff are selected because they have already reached a level of professionalism. They are meticulous about their work and exercise extreme care with attention to details. They are expected to serve but not be seen. They make guests and visitors to the home feel welcomed. Butlers and maids often serve those who have attained a higher education level than them. They carry themselves with deference, respect and esteem.

I can think of one movie in particular where a man served at the highest level of government. He had a family of his own, but he maintained a high level of dedication to his responsibilities. To appear competent, a service worker must be knowledgeable about a variety of things that occur in the world because it reflects well. If a guest engages you in conversation, your response must be sufficient without over-engaging.

It is important to keep your employer's confidence. You hear nothing, you see nothing, You only serve. Their personal lives take a backseat when they are called on assignment. It pays to be resourceful and quick thinking as well as a person of self-discipline.

These are people who serve before their own needs are met. Sometimes, they serve while deeply wounded.

The Parallel of Serving in the Kingdom

The rigors of service make the service industry unappealing. In fact, it may be a turn-off for most people. The Western World categorizes service workers as low-functioning and low-achieving, but we must take note of what's different about serving in The Kingdom.

When you serve in The Kingdom of God, you must serve out of love and not out of obligation. There is a distinct difference. 1 Corinthians 12:31 refers to love as a more excellent way. Serving makes a powerful impact when done in the God kind of love. The world's system tends to use people, and often, they are not paid well. We can think of a host of jobs under this umbrella, such as teachers, police officers, cooks, cashiers, childcare workers, customer service representatives, garbage collectors, etc. But in His Kingdom, God looks out for those who are determined to serve Him. In fact, He says this:

"For God is not unrighteous to forget your work and labour of love, which ye have shewed toward his name, in that ye have ministered to the saints, and do minister."
(Hebrews 6:10)

This scripture lets us know that God will not forget how we've worked for Him, ministering to believers and in soul winning. He is not unjust, and He's not fraudulent to allow you to work for Him and then leave you hanging. God blesses those who serve Him.

The story of the prodigal son in Luke 15 has several strong messages in it. This passage reveals the character of God through the father of the estate. When the prodigal lost everything, he had to resort to eating what the pigs ate. That's when he began to come to his senses.

"And when he came to himself, he said, How many hired servants of my father's have bread enough and to spare, and I perish with hunger!"
(Luke 15:17)

We discover two things that the father provided to his servants:

1. Bread enough
2. And to spare

Bread Enough

How many times have you worked at a job where you were underpaid? Have you worked at a place where the people in management were highly compensated and those doing the main work of the business received wages that didn't even meet their needs? When the prodigal son acknowledged that the servants were being paid "bread enough," he was saying his father was a fair wage employer! A fair wage is an amount of money that an employee receives for their work that meets their basic needs.

Keep in mind that these pay practices were in reference to the servants—not the family members. His dad was a stellar employer because he was paying his servants enough to support their own households without wondering how they were going to make it.

And To Spare

Paying enough is good, but in the second half of his sentence, we find out that the prodigal's father was not only paying enough, but he was also paying "and to spare." Are we talking about over and above? Are we talking about bonus money? Are we talking about discretionary income and the ability to put something aside? Yes, because the grace of giving was on this man. He loved giving to others. Haven't you ever wondered why the prodigal had the gall to ask his father for his inheritance while the man was still living? It's because he had grown up witnessing this grace of giving on his dad. The prodigal saw something that his older brother did not see. In the Church, we haven't seen it yet either, but God takes care of His own.

When we talk about those who walk away from service and shun the hard work, sometimes there are two root strongholds at work. Insecurity and inferiority.

In general, when a person is insecure, it's because they've allowed themselves to be tied up by an emotion that involves lack of confidence and feelings of uncertainty and fear, especially about one's own abilities. While insecurity can cause you to walk away from a number of activities, it will also make you shy away from serving others. Philippians 4:13 tells us "I can do all things through Christ which strengtheneth me." God never asks us to do things in our own human strength, but if we dare to become bold enough to work for Him, He gives supernatural strength in the inner man. In order to get to that place of boldness, you must learn who you are in Christ.

The other stronghold is inferiority, feeling that you are lower in status than others. This was my problem for a large part of my life. I always thought someone else could do it better than I could, that maybe somehow I simply wasn't good enough. I was always waiting for someone to come minister to me that I could serve God with boldness. I was searching for validation. However, the whole time, the Spirit of God was giving me thoughts, hopes and desires to serve Him. These desires were so deeply rooted in me that I couldn't stop fantasizing about serving God in a greater way, but why was no one consistently helping me with this inferiority complex? God didn't want me to be babied. I needed the messages about what it means to be a new creature in Christ Jesus and who I am in Him. Those messages are vital, and I needed to receive them in faith.

While in my thirties, I would go to a friend's house whose mom had suffered a major stroke. We would meet on Saturday mornings and gather around her bed to pray for her mother to be healed and to regain consciousness. We were serious about her recovery, so we were consistent about meeting on a regular basis to pray. Often, after we prayed, there would be tongues and interpretation, but on this one occasion, we waited in the silence, and I heard God speak on the inside of me. I was so surprised at what He said that I had great difficulty believing He was talking to me.

"You are very valuable," He said.

I was shocked. No one had ever said such a thing to me. It shook me, and I wondered what God saw in me that I didn't see. I kept it private. I didn't want to share it with anyone, especially since I couldn't figure out what in the world He was talking about. I was certain no one would understand. I certainly didn't. After all, He didn't say I was valuable. He said I was *very* valuable.

I would remember this from time to time over the years. I would recall the warmth and firmness of His voice speaking to me that day. I knew it was Him--without doubt. I would never have made up something like that. So, these two strongholds, insecurity and inferiority, must be dealt with if we are to go on to greater things. God never meant for you to be insecure. Insecurity comes from the spirit of fear, and we know He did not give us a spirit of fear.

"For God hath not given us the spirit of fear; but of power, and of love, and of a sound mind."
(2 Timothy 1:7)

If this spirit of fear did not come from God, we know it came from our enemy. You must cast it off and not remain in its nasty clutches. It is a hindrance to the furtherance of The Kingdom in the same way that inferiority is. The strongholds of insecurity and inferiority live in the mind. They take up residence in the mind and the emotions in order to limit us, but we have an instruction in the Book of Romans.

> "Be not conformed to this world: but be ye transformed by the renewing of your mind, that ye may prove what is that good, and acceptable, and perfect, will of God."
> (Romans 12:2)

There must be transformation if you will go on to do the greater works God has assigned you. It is your job to become a student of the Word of God, and little by little, bit by bit, your thinking will begin to line up with the reality of who you are in Christ.

Kingdom Assignments – The Short List

After Jesus had arisen from the dead in Mark 16, we see that those who had been with him had taken up a new activity--they were mourning and weeping. They were so engaged in it that when they were told that Jesus had risen from the dead, it sent them into unbelief. They didn't even consider that such a thing could be true. Later, Jesus appeared to the remaining eleven disciples while they were having a meal, and it says He upbraided them for their unbelief and hardness of heart.

Upbraid means to criticize severely and to scold vehemently. I'm telling you, He let them have it. After all they had seen the Master do in his earthly ministry, they still fell into unbelief caused by hardness of heart. Jesus was disappointed and He let them know it! After the shakeup, He gave them instructions because that was still his crew.

"Go ye into all the world, and preach the gospel to every
creature."
(Mark 16:15)

The main assignment to the Church is written in verses fifteen through eighteen.

1. Go into all the world and preach the gospel to every creature
2. They shall cast out devils
3. They shall speak with new tongues
4. They shall take up serpents
5. If they drink anything deadly, it will not harm them
6. They shall lay hands on the sick, and they shall recover

It's important to note that he said signs would follow the preaching and teaching of the Gospel. (See verse 17.) We're not going to skip over that part. If the Church is preaching the gospel, these signs should be following. When the Church is not preaching the gospel, you need not wonder why there are no signs. When someone is looking for a church home, they wonder which one to join and what kind of pastor to follow. As my pastor says, "If signs aren't following you, then why should I?"

The Art of Waiting on God

What is your definition of art? Art is the expression of ideas and emotions through a physical medium like painting, sculpture, film, dance, writing, photography or theatre. Those who love the creative process usually devote their lives to art. Have you ever thought that waiting on God is a creative process? A process that we haven't been taught?

Something happens when we're glad to serve the Lord. Some people's thoughts go to the wild side, and they begin to assume they need to do something extreme in order to serve God. But you don't need to rent a big white truck and start driving through the city with a bullhorn unless that is specifically what God assigned you to do. Instead, what if you begin serving in your local church? During that time, you're learning who God is and you're being developed. You are becoming who God originally intended for you to be. If the teaching is Biblically sound, you'll get full on the inside and begin to tell those around you about His goodness. When transformation begins, something is going to spill out of you.

"Serve the Lord with gladness: come before his presence with singing. Know ye that the Lord he is God: it is he that hath made us, and not we ourselves; we are his people, and the sheep of his pasture."
(Psalm 100:2-3)

When you come before the Lord singing, His presence shows up. It creates capacity on the inside of you, capacity that you didn't know you had. The creative process of worship and praise expands you, and then the hunger begins. A desire to know more about Jehovah begins to grow. He is God. He made us. We didn't make ourselves. He enabled us to be His people and the sheep of His pasture. Why? We give Him so much trouble, so much opposition, why would He even take notice of us when He could just as easily squash all of us with His big toe and find something more satisfying? Are we connected to Him in some way that we haven't discovered?

When we become hungry in this way and begin to come before Him, He sees the hunger, and He begins to feed us with knowledge of the holy, with wisdom and understanding. We begin to see how to function in spiritual things and how to win battles. The first time you realize that solid knowledge of God results in understanding and insight, you know you're hooked for life. The art of waiting on God initiates a process in which we begin to learn of Him, find ways to worship Him and search for ways to serve. Learn, worship, serve.

Let's go through the process. Let's make it an art form. Let's anticipate the outcomes with joy.

Know Your Customer

A waiter who practices excellence in service can serve any customer and make them happy, but have you ever noticed the exchange that takes place when the waiter knows his customer because he or she has served that customer many times? The waiter knows the customer's likes and dislikes, preferences and peculiarities, and he caters to him with the benefit of inside information. There comes a time when the customer asks for that particular waiter by name because they know of his or her dependability, inherent talent and skill.

When that customer orders what he desires from the menu and is satisfied with the service and warm experience he has received, he not only pays, but he tips well. Likewise, so does God. If you study to play the piano as a child, there will be applause from those who love you and your efforts. If, over time, you practice and become skillful, there will be applause on a different level. Aside from applause, there will be such things as awe, enjoyment and invitations to play at the best venues. You become sought after. When you become skillful and dependable in God's eyes, you become sought after. When a high level task needs to be undertaken, He will seek you out, specifically, to execute it.

Do you know Him? Yud Hei Vav Hei. Jehovah. Adonai is a Hebrew word that means Lord, someone with power and authority, someone who rules. The One who was, who is and who will always be. The self-existing one.

> "And God said unto Moses, I Am That I Am: and he said, Thus shalt thou say unto the children of Israel, I Am hath sent me unto you."
> (Exodus 3:14)

It defies the mind to comprehend such a person, yet He makes himself known to us through His Word which contains His will and His ways.

He is all powerful, but He is a God of love, and a father who is longsuffering. Longsuffering means to patiently endure hardship or offense that lasts for a long time. Mankind has given God opposition and offensive behaviors for a very long time. Yet, He is faithful and continues to love us, patiently waiting for us to come into close fellowship with Him. God is so patient, in fact, that over time, the majority of society has mistakenly assumed that His Word is outdated and has no relevance for today. Sin has become non-existent in the minds of many who live their lives according to their own philosophies and feelings. This is why it's important that ministers preach the full gospel because Romans 6:23 lets us know that "the wages of sin is death; but the gift of God is eternal life through Jesus Christ our Lord." The world doesn't understand that there is a wage attached to what God calls sin.

Sometimes that wage is paid during a person's lifetime, and sometimes it's paid when they pass into eternity.

Know your Customer—a God of love but also a God of justice. Those who have a liberal approach to life may think that God is too loving to send anyone to hell. He doesn't send them. People make choices. If you had rules in your house and one child obeyed while the other chose to disobey, the result would be disorder. Would both children receive the same reward? No, because rewards reinforce behavior whether good or bad. In everyday life, some people work while others steal, abuse and murder. Would you be pleased if the thief, abuser and murderer received the same benefits in life while you worked? No, they're on a different reward system. God does not smile at lawlessness.

Here's another characteristic of God. Psalm 145 says God is gracious. Let me describe it this way. I have an aunt and uncle that I've always adored. When we were growing up, we would visit their house regularly, and all the kids in the neighborhood wanted to come over because Auntie loved everybody, including the children. If she gave one a popsicle, she'd make sure every single one got a popsicle. As soon as we entered her house, she would ask if we wanted anything to eat. If we hesitated one eighth of a second, she'd start pulling things out of the refrigerator and preparing something she called "a little bit of nothing." We had food at home, but that gift of hospitality wouldn't allow her to sit down and not serve. And Uncle was always (and still is) smart, quick-witted and fun to be around. I couldn't pronounce his name well (Hosea) when I was a little girl, so I ended up calling him Hi-C. I had bourgeois tendencies even then. I'm telling you they welcomed everybody, and everybody always felt welcome. God is gracious. He is predisposed to welcome us and to show us favor. He is not like Auntie and Uncle. They are like Him. Graciousness is a beautiful gift that comes from God the Father.

"God shall judge the righteous and the wicked."
(Ecclesiastes 3:17)

Although God is gracious, patient, faithful and longsuffering, He is also the Judge of all mankind. Whenever we can warn someone, share with them, or teach, we give them opportunities to know God's plan. How dare we keep it to ourselves.

In the subconscious, many think that God plays favorites or has secrets that He only shares with a favorite few. This is not true. He that seeks finds, but many don't seek. The subconscious is the part of our mental processes that influences our thoughts, emotions and behavior. It's funny how when we don't know enough about God, the mind makes us suspicious of Him. And what do we normally do with suspects? We see them in a negative light. We don't seek open conversations with them. We question them harshly. We don't believe their answers because suspicion demands that we see them as enemies. In our dealings with God, we think He has favorites and that those favorites are the only ones He shares himself with. People play favorites in the workplace, in some families, in governmental systems and other places, but there is no respect of persons with God. (Romans 2:11.) He loves everyone equally.

How many people can you identify in your own life who would give up everything they had, including their ruling status and their own life in order to save you from certain death? Possibly no one, but The Redeemer did this. He created a world with all of its complexities, made people in His own image, and then decided to die in order to save them, to redeem them. If you owned a small piece of land that you purchased for $100,000 and a billionaire came to purchase that land from you for millions, who determined the value of the land? Did you determine the value, or did the billionaire determine the value? The billionaire did. God determined your value when He died for you. He is the Redeemer who we must get to know. When we get to know Him better, we will serve Him better.

Know your Customer. Pursue Him. Allow Him to show you how to serve.

CHAPTER 4
A WARFARE TESTIMONY

I lost my well-paying job in October of 2018, and I lasted financially for another six months. Afterwards, the COVID pandemic reared its ugly head, and I didn't find another job aside from food delivery. Eventually, I lost the condo that I had paid the mortgage on for 16 years and had to move home with my parents to sleep on the sofa, the only space available for me. Having no job, I had no responsibilities other than to help care for my aging parents. However, one Saturday morning in July, I got up, took a shower, got dressed and sat down on that sofa wondering, "What am I supposed to be doing today?" There were no plans, and I had nowhere to go, but that question plagued me as if I was supposed to be somewhere doing something. Soon, a hysterical phone call came in answer to the question that was nagging my spirit.

I jumped into my car and broke the speed limit getting to my daughter's house to take her to the local hospital where they had rushed her husband. He was in respiratory distress, which meant he could not breathe. Because of the pandemic, the first thing hospital staff assumed was that he had contracted the COVID virus. They tested him several times, and each time, the test came back negative, but he was declining rapidly. They had to administer oxygen because he could not breathe on his own. This hospital was unable to help because they knew this was a complex case. The decision was made to transfer this able-bodied young man who often worked six to seven days a week to a large, well-known teaching hospital thirty minutes away. Several family members were assembled in the parking lot of the hospital, refusing to go home. We watched a huge yellow helicopter board him and whisk him away to a more well-equipped facility. We believe he had a stroke when he was airlifted.

In addition to respiratory distress, the diagnoses were beginning to stack up even though those diagnoses had not been communicated to us.

I was glad he was going to the big teaching hospital because I believed they had more resources and would be able to help him. The second hospital also tested for COVID, and each test came back negative. Although we didn't understand the root issue, we left late into the night, confidently expecting that a hospital of that size, with that reputation, staff and knowledge would figure it out. The next morning, I began to pace the floor of my daughter's house, talking to God, and seeking direction because I needed to know the appropriate strategy and battle plan. Engage in prayer or let the situation unfold until the doctors could give us precise information? When I sensed that this was a battle I needed to undertake, I told the Lord "I need someone to help me." I knew this was a formidable situation, and I had never faced a battle of this magnitude. When a human body cannot breathe, it dies.

My first mindset was to refuse panic and despair. Outright!

COVID was a time of quarantine, but God answered my prayer quickly as one of my daughter's relatives walked into the dining room of her house. I was on a Zoom call. As she walked up behind me, I heard her begin to pray in the Spirit. Relief came over me because an emergency situation is not the time to teach anyone how to become skillful in prayer. My daughter's cousin Laverne knew the Word of God. She already had a strong prayer life, and she was bold in prayer! I didn't need someone who would shrink back in doubt and fear because of the seriousness of the situation. I also didn't need anyone whose best course of action was to pray those "if it be thy will" type of prayers. I needed someone who would stand up like a grizzly, ten toes down and stand their ground in the spirit realm.

It was Sunday, and a new phone call came. It was the hospital asking us to return to the facility as soon as possible. They were honest enough to say they wanted to have an end-of-life conversation with us. For years, I had wanted to find one of those racetracks that allowed drivers to speed as fast as they dared around the track for thrills and bragging rights. I never proactively sought one out, but that day, several drivers in our family, including me, set the highway on fire. Thank God the police didn't stop us.

I don't know how we all got past the security desk when only one person was allowed to visit a patient during the pandemic. I credit it to God and to the actions of one family member who had people skills. She dealt with the security personnel at the front desk, and we found ourselves (about seven or eight of us) in a conference room with a tiny, young female doctor who sat with us and explained what they had discovered and why they wanted to allow us time to decide to take him off life support.

The doctor discussed the diagnoses for my son-in-law:

1. Respiratory distress
2. Blood clots in the brain, chest and legs
3. Stroke
4. Pulmonary embolism
5. Paralysis on his left side
6. Posterior fossa hemorrhage

Do you remember the old western television show "Bonanza" where one of the characters was Hoss Cartwright? The actor's name was Dan Blocker. He died of a pulmonary embolism, but my son-in-law not only had that but other life-threatening issues.

May We Have This Room

After the doctor quietly explained everything that had occurred to his body, she let us know that there was nothing they could do. The brain stem damage alone was enough to demonstrate that they had reached the limits of what they could do. There was no way to reverse the "stacked attack" damage that had been done to his body, not to mention the fact that he was one hundred percent dependent on oxygen and had no ability to breathe on his own. The room was thick with silence and a tinge of despair. The doctor asked if anyone had any questions. Being the polite Southern girl that I am, I waited to allow others to go first with questions, but no one did. That's when I raised my hand.

"I have a question. May we have this room?"

She answered yes and left us. I have been in love with God since I was a girl, and after all the things the devil had done in my life—the lack of good teaching, marriage to someone I was not compatible with, the devastation of divorce, the stress of being a single parent, the financial struggle, the lack of emotional support and shouldering the load all on my own, followed by job loss and being evicted from my home—I WAS READY FOR A FIGHT!

So, in that small room, we began to pray. I ripped Satan a new one, making sure he knew that I knew my rights in Christ. As we began to pray the Word of God over Kam, I suddenly realized where we were. We were in the Courts of Heaven pleading this young man's case to God. If we didn't, he would surely die. After two hours of fervent warfare prayer, the room went quiet. I began to listen, expecting God to speak. The prayer partner that God had sent walked over to my chair and quietly spoke a scripture.

"He shall deliver you from the snare of the fowler."
(Psalm 91:3)

To this day, she does not remember doing or saying that. A snare is a trap set to catch animals and to disable them from escaping a painful death.

When there was no tongues and interpretation and no word of prophecy, I opened my eyes and looked up toward the ceiling. I had never in my life seen anything like it, but into the hospital came an extremely speedy gold chariot with precious jewels decorating the sides. In that golden chariot were two angels, both tall and slender. One angel was shorter than the other, and they were both smiling big smiles. This is a comical observation, but they looked like geeks, the kid you went to school with who always studied, always obeyed his parents and did everything well. They seemed to be very pleased with our intercession. As they stepped off the chariot, each angel held a huge, golden, liquid ball larger than a beach ball. Both liquid balls were pulsating and bubbling, and I knew they had brought healing and that Kam would live.

In life-threatening situations, people generally fall apart, feeling helpless. They give in and accept defeat. Even in the Christian community, when a believer has not developed their prayer life or does not know their rights in Christ or how to get answers from God, they fall apart as well. I'm not saying I didn't have a moment of emotionalism during this tenuous event. I did, but I reigned it in. I made a conscious decision to reign it in because I know The Most High God. I took charge of my emotions because I was ready to deliver a blow to the enemy, whatever that blow looked like. I made my emotions take a backseat because I had sat learning the Word of God in a Bible teaching church for over 30 years. I reigned it in because the Word of God either works or it doesn't. I decided to fight because I've got Back-Up, baby! I was unable to excuse myself from having been taught that He's the God of the impossible. His Word says that we are to come boldly to the throne of grace. So, with as much boldness as I could, that's what I did.

I was so sure about it that toward the end of our prayer time, I was on the verge of saying to God, "If You don't get him up, I'm coming up there (heaven), and we're going to talk about this face to face." I know that sounds obnoxious and even disrespectful, but I guarantee you God respected my boldness and was pleased with our faith. Before uttering those words, I looked up and saw the two angels come into the hospital on that gold chariot. I cannot tell you how shocked I was. I wasn't shocked that God would answer. I was shocked that He sent a high-speed, decked out vehicle from heaven with two angels whose faces displayed the fact that God the Father was pleased with us. I was hesitant to tell anyone about it for a long time. I didn't want anyone to think I was cuckoo for cocoa puffs.

The next day, the hospital called to say, "Well, we don't know what happened, but he's no longer one hundred percent dependent on oxygen. He's down to about ninety percent." The next day, "He's only eighty percent dependent on the oxygen." And on it went until he was less and less dependent on oxygen and began to breathe fully on his own. The hospital never understood why he began to improve, and in time, they asked permission to do a case study on him for learning purposes. They could do all the studying they wanted. The answers they sought were never going to be found in his medical records, lab tests or the surgeries that they were finally able to do once he began to recover his health. I had seen my first miracle up close and personal!

When he began to improve, doctors discovered that he had been born with a hole in his heart. A large hole in the heart can send extra blood to the lungs and cause the right side of the heart to work too hard. Without treatment, the right side of the heart grows larger over time and becomes weak. The blood pressure in the arteries can also increase, causing pulmonary hypertension. The enemy had been trying to take this man out since the day he was born, but now he has a "dead man walking" testimony. You don't come back from blood clots in the brain, chest and legs, a stroke, pulmonary embolism, posterior fossa hemorrhage, paralysis, respiratory distress and a hole in the heart without supernatural intervention. It's not happenstance. When you move the hand of God with faith, you get supernatural results. But you cannot pray that way if you do not know the Word of God or how faith works.

I'm not boasting about what happened here. What I'm saying is that if you accept Jesus as your savior, learn His Word, get some spiritual training, develop a prayer life and make yourself available to serve Him, He will put you at the right place at the right time to do His will and see great exploits.

CHAPTER 5
EQUIPMENT AND
TRAINING

The purpose of sharing Kam's "dead man walking" testimony is to encourage you to know who you are in Christ and to become educated about the Word of God so that you are equipped to do the works God assigns you to do. The Christian community doesn't need even one more flim flam man or woman operating in the Body of Christ. We need those who have dedicated themselves to learning about their Creator and His ways. These are the people who will execute God-given assignments instead of making up their own. It is my hope that this testimony will whet your appetite for the things God is longing to do. When I was walking around my daughter's house praying, one of the first things I did was to ask God "Do I fight this battle, or is it too far gone?" When I got the peace of God to go into battle, I went ready!

You can go ready, too, once you're prepared and have your orders from heaven. I want to touch on some fundamental things that equip us to be effective for The Kingdom of God and make us fit for the Master's use. I won't go into them in-depth. If there's a piece of equipment in this chapter that you're unfamiliar with, you'll hear me say over and over again, "Go back to the learning environment" because the purpose of this book is to encourage you to serve God and to practice giving Him maximum effort. This book is written to God's Remnant who have compassion for a lost and dying world full of hurting people. The Remnant is a group of people whose love for God runs "inner core deep," and they'll do anything He tells them to do. Inner core is like the layers of the earth. On top is the crust. Further down is the mantle, followed by the outer core. At the center is the inner core. The inner core burns hot. Are you burning hot for Jehovah?

The Remnant is a group of people who cannot run off to heaven and leave others to perish in ignorance. They know that many mistakenly believe that "I'm a good person" is the plan of salvation, but this is deceptive. The Remnant doesn't decide that people should have figured it out on their own. Did you figure out the plan of salvation on your own? No, you did not. You had help that redirected you out of eternal hell fire and into the family of God. Don't be ashamed if your interest in the lost has waned. Hop on YouTube and watch a few NDE (near death experience) videos. These videos will help you regain your focus. They are very, very sobering.

What Is A New Creature?

This chapter is about equipment and training, so I want to begin by addressing the question "What is being saved?" Some call it being born again or becoming a believer. What is a new creature?

"Therefore if any man be in Christ, he is a new creature: old things are passed away; behold, all things are become new.
(2 Corinthians 5:17)

This scripture tells us that when we open our mouths and accept Jesus as Lord and Savior—and we do it because it's a heart motivated decision and not something rote—we are born again. We become a new creature, a person that never existed before. You see yourself in the mirror following that decision, that prayer, and you look the same. How are you a new creature that never existed before? Because you are more than the physical body that you see in the mirror each day. There are three parts to you. You are a spirit, you have a soul (mind, will, emotions, intellect), and you live in a body. Your spirit became born again the moment you released your faith to receive Jesus into your heart.

The next step is transformation by having your mind renewed. In other words, you need to learn who you are, what kingdom you belong to, and how to operate in that kingdom. There is no such thing as living a successful Christian life without being educated. If you lack the necessary education, you will remain conformed to the world's destructive ways of doing life.

When I was a teenager, my church took the youth out to knock on doors in the neighborhood and ask for canned goods during the Thanksgiving season. The church used the canned goods for the Thanksgiving meals they distributed to the needy. Well, me being me, I had a "wild" idea and posed it to one of the adults. "Why can't we witness to the people when they come to the door?" I asked, because that's what I wanted to learn how to do. "You're too young," I was told. You ask for canned goods and we'll do the witnessing. I respect leadership. I didn't ask again.

What thinking individual would deny a willing and ready teen the opportunity to learn how to win someone to Christ? We need huge adjustments in our thinking so that we can move forward. Maybe you've never been trained in soul winning but desire to learn. As I said before, this book is not in-depth training; however, I'm going to give you six scriptures you can use to share the gospel. You may not use all six at one encounter with a person. You may use only one—whatever the Holy Spirit leads you to do.

THE NEED

"Wherefore, as by one man sin entered into the world, and death by sin; and so death passed upon all men, for that all have sinned."
(Romans 5:12)

THE SOLUTION

"For God so loved the world, that he gave his only begotten Son, that whosoever believeth in him should not perish, but have everlasting life."
(John 3:16)

THE NAME OF THE SOLUTION

Be it known unto you all, and to all the people of Israel, that by the name of Jesus Christ of Nazareth, whom ye crucified, whom God raised from the dead, even by him doth this man stand here before you whole. This is the stone which was set at nought of you builders, which is become the head of the corner. Neither is there salvation in any other: for there is none other name under heaven given among men, whereby we must be saved.
(Acts 4:10-12)

HOW TO APPLY THE SOLUTION

But what saith it? The word is nigh thee, even in thy mouth, and in thy heart: that is, the word of faith, which we preach; That if thou shalt confess with thy mouth the Lord Jesus, and shalt believe in thine heart that God hath raised him from the dead, thou shalt be saved. For with the heart man believeth unto righteousness; and with the mouth confession is made unto salvation.
(Romans 10:8-10)

SALVATION IS A GIFT

"For by grace are ye saved through faith; and that not of yourselves: it is the gift of God. Not of works, lest any man should boast."
(Ephesians 2:8-9)

YOU HAVE THE RIGHT TO RECEIVE THIS GIFT

As many as received him, to them gave he power to become the sons of God, even to them that believe on his name.
(John 1:12)

One thing that should touch our hearts deeply is the blindness factor. Satan is called the god of this world because Adam committed high treason against God and defaulted his ruling position to satan. Second Corinthians chapter 4 informs us that the god of this world has blinded the minds of those who do not believe. It is our duty to pray for them and to witness to them as opportunity presents itself. Blindness is a horrid debilitation physically. Spiritual blindness is also a horrid debilitation, but this blindness has eternal consequences attached to it.

"But if our gospel be hid, it is hid to them that are lost. In whom the god of this world hath blinded the minds of them which believe not, lest the light of the glorious gospel of Christ, who is the image of God, should shine unto them."
(2 Corinthians 43-4)

The Power of the Word

The majority of the Christian world has not been taught about the power that's resident in the Word of God. We have a measure of respect for the Bible, but we have yet to discover the power in it. I don't know if I was an odd child or not, but I watched certain things more than others. For instance, I was highly curious about leadership. My questions were "Who gets to be in charge and why? Is a leader made over time, or are they born that way--with a natural authority?" I've found answers along the way to some of these questions, but I was watching intensely. I watched my own father give orders, and people would obey. I'm not just talking about in the home. It was in the workplace and sometimes in the neighborhood as well. If he said something to you, you were—shall I say--inclined to obey. I was captivated by this natural gifting and the fact that spoken words could produce compliance.

Would you like to see this type of authority on a much higher level? Let's go over to the first chapter of Genesis. This is the story of creation. Have you ever noticed or counted how many times the text says, "And God said?" For each thing He wanted done, He spoke. He was giving commands in a way similar yet far superior to the way I just described my earthly father operating in his natural leadership gifting. When God speaks, it must come to pass. There is no power shortage with God.

"So shall my word be that goeth forth out of my mouth: it shall not return unto me void, but it shall accomplish that which I please, and it shall prosper in the thing whereto I sent it."
(Isaiah 55:11)

When God speaks, it must happen, and similarly, when we speak the Word of God, it must come to pass. Of course, it must be done in faith, but it will come to pass. We are sitting on a huge barrel of power because we don't understand what has been handed to us. If you need to know more about the power that's in the Word, please go back to the learning environment so that you can be properly equipped.

Developing Faith (The Access Code)

"Therefore being justified by faith, we have peace with God through our Lord Jesus Christ. By whom also we have access by faith into this grace wherein we stand, and rejoice in hope of the glory of God."
(Romans 5:1-2)

I love talking about the access code, and I love mentioning the access code when I pray. It reminds me that I have a right to approach the throne of God with boldness. It reminds me that I have the right to receive the grace of God and His miracle working power. The dictionary defines access as permission, liberty or ability to enter or approach.

The access code is faith in what He has already shown us in His Word. God will do what He said he would do, but it is impossible to please Him without faith. Faith unlocks things and brings answers. It's the secret weapon of the Christian community, but many don't know how to use it or where it comes from. Again, this chapter is about equipment and training. If you are part of God's Remnant, you probably have already gotten your feet wet concerning faith and you're ready to move forward in your "God assignments." Others will be sparked by this book and by this holy fire movement so that they can begin to touch others in their sphere of influence.

In the testimony of my son-in-law, I stepped into the boldest level of faith I had ever stepped into. I decided within myself that the Word of God is either legitimate or it's not. It either works, or it doesn't. It either has power, or it doesn't. It's either for every generation, or it's not. I was done with the wondering and the hoping and the hesitancy and the hedging. When you hedge on something, you limit or qualify it with conditions and exceptions. We limit and qualify God all the time with conditions and exceptions so that we don't get judged for taking the route called faith. We hear our faith limits when we say things like "God needed another flower in heaven," or "Well, you never know what the will of the Lord is." The most impactful thing I can tell you is DEAD MAN WALKING!!!

"Now faith is the substance of things hoped for, the evidence of things not seen.
(Hebrews 11:1)

Faith is a spiritual substance, and it produces things you cannot see with the natural eye. Faith is something we must become proficient in.

Righteousness & Authority

You may have heard a Christian, proud, with their chest stuck out saying, "There's none righteous. No, not one." In and of oneself, no, you are not righteous. To gain clarity on the topic of righteousness, you must understand that all of your sin was put on Christ on the cross. You were unrighteous, but He died for you. It was the great exchange, and you became the righteousness of God.

"For he hath made him to be sin for us, who knew no sin; that we might be made the righteousness of God in him." (2 Corinthians 5:21)

So that you don't shy away from this, let's further define it. Simply put, it means right standing with God. Right standing is a phrase that means you have a favorable reputation, or you are in a proper position. Before Christ came, we did not have a favorable reputation with God. We had de-evolved into a bunch of sidewinders full of venom and selfishness. After Adam committed high treason against the Creator, we became rapists, murderers, liars, thieves, uncivilized and lacking in principles, morals and character.

But look at how God approached our contemptible status. Picture this. Your mother takes you to the playground for a fun time, and you start off on the slide. You enjoy the seesaw and the monkey bars, but when mom isn't looking, you find your way to that large circle of reddish-brown mud she told you not to go near. And you revel in it because it's fun, and because it was forbidden. It was big fun until you see the look of horror on her face and know that you're in undeniable trouble, the kind of trouble that you need help getting out of. You know that if only you had a friend, an advocate, you could be saved from the coming wrath.

This is what God did when He looked at us. We were ick on a stick, but He still said "That one is Mine. I can rebuild them. I have the technology. I can make them better than they were before. I can take them from unclean to clean. I can bring them back from death to life. I can make them new again."

And that's exactly what He did. There was a handwriting of ordinances against us because of sin. When Adam trespassed, sin entered, and the glory departed from mankind. But God put Jesus, the only righteous one, on the cross in our place, and HE BLOTTED IT OUT! When He blotted it out, we became righteous the moment we accepted Jesus as savior and lord. We now have an excellent position with God. We can come into His presence anytime we want to. We've been made righteous.

"And you, being dead in your sins and the uncircumcision of your flesh, hath he quickened together with him, having forgiven you all trespasses. Blotting out the handwriting of ordinances that was against us, which was contrary to us, and took it out of the way, nailing it to his cross."
(Colossians 2:13-14)

Righteousness gives you the right to operate in power on the earth, and we must learn how to use that power. Without fear. You already know what I'm going to say. If you don't have in-depth teaching on this topic, please go back to the learning environment and get equipped. You will need to know how to use your authority.

Prayer Life

In order to pray effectively, it is imperative that you know the Word of God and be well versed in it. Otherwise, how will you know what to pray? It cannot be off the top of your head based on your own desires, thoughts or suppositions. It cannot be separate from the will of God, which is the Word of God.

The Word covers every situation you will encounter on this earth, and when you don't know how to pray specifically, the Holy Spirit will direct you. (See John 16:13.)

Now, let's get to this business of praying in other tongues because this is a major piece of equipment. It is the doorway to the supernatural.

In the first chapter of Acts, we see Jesus instructing the disciples to wait for the outpouring and baptism of the Holy Ghost. On the day of Pentecost, they waited as He had instructed them, and there was a powerful outpouring. If you can point out a scripture that clearly indicates that praying in tongues or praying in the spirit has passed away, please let the rest of us know. In the meantime, let me give you a little more insight into its purpose.

Imagine listening to a radio station, and of course, each station operates on a specific frequency. If you're not on that frequency, you will not have access to what is being broadcast. When you pray in tongues, satan does not have access to what you are praying. The language you speak is supernatural, and it is directed to God. When we pray in tongues, we send messages to heaven, and we bypass the limitations of our natural minds.

> "For he that speaketh in an unknown tongue speaketh not unto men, but unto God: for no man understandeth him; howbeit in the spirit he speaketh mysteries."
> (1 Corinthians 14:2)

James 5:16 speaks about prayer in general. The writer said it makes tremendous power available to solve whatever issue is confronting you. The power that is generated applies to praying in your known language as well as praying in the spirit.

"The effectual fervent prayer of a righteous
man availeth much."
(James 5:16)

Praying in tongues produces immense power, capable of breaking chains and shifting spiritual atmospheres. Who would say "no" to having a weapon so powerful that it bypasses restrictions and limitations? When a doctor says there's nothing else they can do, that's a limitation. When an unwieldy neighbor refuses to talk about a compromise, that's a restriction and a limitation. When a teen decides to live an ungodly lifestyle, they're walking into deception that will cost them precious time. When you don't have direction about what to do next in life, it feels like a closed door where all opportunity has been capped off. When someone tells you you cannot enroll for classes because you haven't paid tuition, that exposes a financial limitation. I don't know about you, but I don't enjoy being told no.

"For this people's heart is waxed gross, and their ears are dull
of hearing, and their eyes they have closed; lest at any time
they should see with their eyes and hear with their ears, and
should understand with their heart, and should be converted,
and I should heal them."
(Matthew 13:15)

Jesus was talking about the Jewish people in this passage, but the same concept applies to a great many in the Christian community. Praying in tongues is a major piece of equipment that we need in this hour, but many have closed their eyes and ears to it. If you want to be grandma who got run over by a reindeer, then turn your nose up at this type of prayer and turn your back on this gift, but you've been informed that God has made this supernatural tool available to you.

In 2023, I became displeased that my life was going nowhere. It felt as if a heavy, black canopy had been dropped over the top of me, preventing forward movement. I didn't understand how I had become a prisoner with no way of escape. One weekend, I went to YouTube and for some reason, began to search for videos on praying in other tongues. It wasn't new to me, but for some reason I searched this topic. The next day was Sunday, and at church, Pastor MJ announced to the church that he wanted the congregation to spend the month of January disciplining themselves to pray in the spirit for at least thirty minutes each day. (This is one way to know you have an anointed pastor. The Spirit of God begins leading you a certain way, and when you get to church, the pastor confirms it.) I took the challenge even though I was accustomed to spending more than an hour praying. At first, I spent an hour, then two hours a day. I was determined to know the next step in my life, so I found myself praying three hours a day—one hour early in the morning; another hour at midday and then a third hour before retiring for the night. I don't know how to adequately explain it, but the dark canopy was dissipating, and I knew it. Around April of that year, the Spirit of God began to speak to me about The Art of Waiting on God. I knew it was Him whispering what to jot down. He would even wake me from a sound sleep in the early hours of the morning and give me more ideas, words and phrases. It was my job to do the writing. The anointing was so heavy at times that I would sit and cry. Everyone who knows me knows that I don't enjoy crying, but

I was overcome. That's how this book was birthed—through praying it out first. I'm sure some of you will pick up on the fact that I was praying hoping God would make my life better. Instead, He gave me a job to do. It's funny, but that's how He operates.

When I shared with you the testimony of how we prayed fervently for Kam, I left out another powerful testimony that began in that hospital conference room. Piled into that small conference room was a young man named Lamar and his wife who were relatives of my daughter. They didn't have the developed prayer life that others had, but they possessed a strong loyalty to family, and they refused to leave the hospital in the middle of a family crisis. I adore people like that. They stuck together and were sitting on a small sofa in the room. You need people like this in your life, people who will not budge! Some don't budge in the natural. Others don't budge in the spiritual. Both groups are powerful people because they will stick it out come hell or high water.

The more we prayed, the more emboldened I became. I didn't understand it back then, but I understand now that God uses me in the seeing gift where I see things in the spirit. Seeing that huge gold chariot speed into the hospital was not the first thing I saw that day. I looked over at this young man and I saw light going up and down his arms. I was so charged up that I felt that I was supposed to go over to him and run my hands from his shoulders down his arms, imitating what I saw the light doing. But I stopped myself from doing that. Our main focus was Kam, so I rationalized that I was just being overly emotional, trying to save the world now. My conservative personality stopped me, short-circuited me and kept me from

48

obeying what I felt led to do by the Spirit of God. But I thank God that He gave this young man a life-saving miracle thirteen weeks later because prayer produces power. Here is Lamar's testimony in his own words:

"Last year on this date at 3:09 a.m., some young dudes tried to take me out the game!!!! In the middle of trying to steal one of my kid's cars from in front of my house, five shots were thrown my way in total, one of which missed my head by a matter of inches. Three bypassed me altogether, and one hit me. At that point, seconds felt like hours! I was as calm as I possibly could be, so calm that my wife didn't believe me when I said I was shot. Whole time, I was preventing myself from going into shock and passing out! The ambulance took forever to get to me. Got to the trauma center and it looked like a scene from the movies/tv shows. About seven to eight people were working on me and all I was doing was cracking jokes, masking my fear while still remaining calm to prevent from going into shock or passing out. A year later, I'm still here to tell this story. I'm constantly in pain but still keep a smile on my face. When people ask me how I'm doing, I say I'm fine! The rain and cold be tearing me up!! The nerve damage is a whole other monster. Doctor's visits after doctor's visits, neurology appointments after neurology appointments, but I'm alive and amongst the living!!! And to this very day the surgeon, my nurse practitioner, my primary doctor, and my occupational therapist can't explain how a 40-caliber bullet ended up in a spot where "without a doubt was supposed to shatter bones, break nerves, hit an artery and bleed out." But yet, it somehow bypassed all of that and lodged right in the middle of a nerve and an inch from an artery. They called it a medical miracle. I say the best way I can explain it to you is long story short, God saved my life."

Lamar was shot in the arm—the arm I refused to run my hands down in obedience to what I saw in the spirit realm that day. Dear ones, we need to know the Word of God, but we also need to learn the ways of God. I am sorry that I did not obey what God showed me that day. I will always wonder if I had let go of uncertainty and obeyed if Lamar would have been spared that physical trauma. I tear up every time I think about this incident and my lack of obedience. Many of us attend church because in the back of our minds, it's our hell insurance. But we don't walk in the power of God or know how to cooperate with the move of God. We walk in self-imposed limitations.

In the last seventy-five-plus years, a new group of people has emerged. They attend church in order to learn the Word of God, and they walk in a measure of the power of God. They have a mindset to learn the Word, and they leave in order to practice what they've learned. They desire both. A new breed is on the horizon. So, I apologize to you, Lamar. I WILL become more educated in spiritual things as well as more obedient, but just know that there is still opportunity for you to be completely healed.

Casting Out Devils

"And these signs shall follow them that believe; In my name shall they cast out devils; they shall speak with new tongues."
(Mark 16:17)

This is one of the instructions Jesus gave before he left for heaven. We must be trained in how to do it. I haven't had to cast out a devil, but I remember being in the airport during my business travel days and I saw a young person traveling alone repeating the same phrases over and over while waiting for the plane to arrive at the gate. He was not bothering anybody, but it was obvious that something was wrong. During that period of my life I was not prepared to deal with anything like that. In fact, I decided that if they let that person on the plane, I could wait for the next flight. No reason to rush home.

Today, I'm a different person. I'm willing to learn how to cast out devils because I'm no longer intimidated by an enemy that Jesus knocked out on his own territory. Want to fight, devil? Let's roll because I'll cut your gonads off. You're not reproducing death and loss over here. I've been through too much!

Laying Hands On the Sick

These signs shall follow them that believe:

"They shall lay hands on the sick, and they shall recover."
(Mark 16:18)

We must spend enough time fellowshipping with God and meditating on His Word that the power of it rises up on the inside of us. Meditating the Word of God and spending time with the Healer himself causes that power to rise up in your spirit. Then when you lay hands on the sick, you transmit that power to their bodies by faith, a healing flow of virtue.

One of the things that will accelerate your faith for healing is when you get healed yourself. Over ten years ago, I began to experience horrible hip pain. It was beginning to limit my mobility. At that time, I worked in sales support, and as anyone knows, when you work in sales, you have to show some energy, and you have to keep up with the sales executive. The pain began to feel crippling, not to mention embarrassing. I went to the doctor, who took x-rays and suggested several treatment methods to alleviate the pain. None of those treatments appealed to me. Then it occurred to me that everyone has smart phones (we call them cell phones now), but I wondered if anyone was being smart about how to use them. I began to make my phone work on my behalf by setting three alarms every single day. When each alarm sounded, I would take two to three minutes to speak healing scriptures over my body. A year later, I returned to the same doctor with new x-rays. He wanted to review my case. (By the time of the appointment, the pain had disappeared.)

It took a while, but when he returned to the exam room, he began bowing at the hip, his arms extended in praise, with the new x-rays in one hand. I wondered "What is wrong with this dude?" He put the x-rays up on the board and smiled at me as he said, "I don't know what you've been doing, but look at this." He made several marks on the new x-rays highlighting a small c-curve on my skeletal structure at the hip. God had placed a little tea cup handle on the side where the pain had been! I don't know anyone else who has a little tea cup handle on their skeletal structure, but at some point, I'll place the picture on my website at www.delilahspivey.com so that you can see it for yourself. Walking with God is exciting. We cannot keep knowledge of Him to ourselves. It's wonderful for me to have tea with The Most High God, but we must go beyond the "us four and no more" mentality and begin to touch those around us.

Gifts of the Spirit

God has given us gifts. We don't employ them at will, but 1 Corinthians 12:7 says the gifts are given to us so that we can benefit from them. What are those gifts?

"For to one is given by the Spirit the word of wisdom; to another the word of knowledge by the same Spirit. To another faith by the same Spirit; to another the gifts of healing by the same Spirit. To another the working of miracles; to another prophecy; to another discerning of spirits; to another divers kinds of tongues; to another the interpretation of tongues."
(I Corinthians 12:8-10)

When I was a young, divorced mom, I worked at a mental hospital in an area of Detroit that had been beautiful and fabulous back in the day. At the time I worked in that corridor near Wayne State University, there were many poor people who walked the streets--those with addictions, the homeless and mental patients who drove the recidivism rate because they stayed out of hospital only long enough to qualify to return there. I was afraid of many of those people, not understanding the roots of what brought them to unfavorable places in life. I worked for the President and COO, and I would leave the office clutching my purse and walking quickly to the employee parking lot which was about a block away. At times, it seemed like the longest city block in the world. I always hoped I would not encounter any of the former patients because they were frightening.

One day, I was speed walking to the parking lot when I saw a tall, overweight girl who was crying as if she had lost all hope in life. She was sitting on the steps of an abandoned building which made me hurry even more. "That's another one of the patients," I assumed. And because she was a big girl, I knew she could take me down if she had a mind to. But then I heard the voice of the Holy Spirit. He told me that she had run out of money and couldn't take the bus back home. At that point, I was faced with a choice. Do I believe that I had heard from God, or do I pick up speed and run to my vehicle? That day, I chose to believe I had heard from God, and I walked down the long walkway of that building to approach her. I asked her what was wrong. She explained that she had been looking for a job and had to pay more bus fares than she had anticipated. I asked her if she believed God, and she said yes, she was trying to have faith for someone to help her. She wasn't going from person to person asking for money. She was just sitting there distraught, her whole face wet with tears, operating in faith the best she knew how. I admonished her to never give up when believing God, gave her more money than she needed to get home and sent her on her way. I don't believe in giving just enough. Leave that for the penny pinchers. I believe in giving over and above. I could tell she was very relieved. Side note: sometimes when you're making an effort to have faith in God, you may still be crying like you've been whipped but keep making strides until you become strong in faith. Let there be no shame to your game. Your progress in spiritual things is extremely important.

I had been given a word of knowledge by the Spirit of God, and I trusted Him enough to act on it and be a blessing to a stranger in need. I was making strides myself. Here is a list of the gifts in First Corinthians chapter twelve:

1. Word of wisdom
2. Word of knowledge
3. Special faith
4. Gifts of healing
5. Working of miracles
6. Prophecy
7. Discerning of spirits
8. Diverse kinds of tongues
9. Interpretation of tongues

We must become educated about these nine gifts that God gives and cast fear away so that we can operate in them when He gives us the manifestation of that gift. We cannot be ill-equipped at this point in history when the winds of darkness are blowing like tornadoes, hurricanes and monsoons. God is looking for those He can use at this critical time. There is an elite team all over the earth, a team that has been trained in the Word and in the ways of God. They are The Remnant. If you haven't been properly educated about the gifts of the Spirit, you know what to do. Learning Environment 101.

CHAPTER 6
DAILY FUNCTION

The Spirit Realm

They lied to us, y'all. They told us that outer space was the next great frontier, the place where we would find all the newest challenges and room for development, exploration and expansion. Outer space is definitely the place where most men haven't gone before, but there's another space, another realm that is rich with adventure, discovery and great victories. Creation is waiting for us to take our places there.

We've been taught to cater to the mind, the will, the emotions, the intellect and the body, but we greatly neglect our spirits. We don't feed the spirit man the type of food it needs to become strong. The spirit is the main part of us, the part that lives on after leaving the physical body. When the spirit man is fed the proper diet consistently, it will develop into a place of prominence versus how we normally live our lives by developing our minds and/or our bodies to achieve goals. We work our way through grade school so that we can function in society. Others go on to college and other higher levels of education, esteeming academia as the way to high achievement. You've also witnessed people develop their bodies to get to a place of high achievement in sports. While there is nothing wrong with developing the mind or the body, it is the spirit that suffers from malnutrition and becomes developmentally disabled.

When you do not develop your spirit, your ability to communicate and interact with the Creator of the Universe is impaired. The good news is that it doesn't have to be impaired for the duration of your life. You can be fed, nourished, and developed to do great things in the earth. Although The Art of Waiting on God is not written to Christians who are young in the things of God or those who are satisfied with their undercover walk with the Lord, this is still a word of encouragement to the babes in Christ. The main goal of this book is to speak to God's Remnant and bring them to a focal point of readiness and active service. Do something for God every week, every day if the opportunity is there, but especially if you've received instruction from Him.

Many who began their journey with the Lord, ready to learn of Him and to do great things, have fallen apathetic. Apathy has taken them to a place of having or showing little or no interest, concern or emotion. Having little interest gives way to selfishness, and this has made us dormant.

Did you at one time have great zeal for Jesus and were unafraid if anyone noticed it? Were you cautioned to calm that zeal down by a fellow church member who thought you needed to stay in your place? Did they dampen your enthusiasm for witnessing to the lost, laying hands on the sick, seeing the gifts of the Spirit operate or seeing signs and wonders? Usually, it's people who have been short-circuited who will short-circuit others. They will dampen your enthusiasm because someone or something dampened theirs. It's this kind of behavior that kills momentum and movement in the Body of Christ.

Dormancy is a place of being asleep, inactive and sluggish. But that day is over! We are pulling back into our prayer closets to spend time in the Presence of God to be empowered and to receive our assignments.

One thing that will motivate us to return to the prayer closet is compassion.

"And when the day was now far spent, his disciples came unto him, and said, This is a desert place, and now the time is far passed. Send them away that they may go into the country round about, and into the villages, and buy themselves bread: for they have nothing to eat. He answered and said unto them give ye them to eat."
(Mark 16:35-37)

What the Church has been doing in this day and age is exactly what the disciples advised Jesus to do. "Send them away." We send them away to social agencies, to hospitals, to street corners and to food banks, and still the people are hungry. We send them away, where they ultimately find themselves disconnected from God and in hell because they never received the one meal they were truly longing for—the Bread of Life.

Do you know what the stark contrast is between earth and hell? While living on earth, we can still hope. We can have expectations and desires for a better life. In hell, there is no hope!

We must be about our Father's business. You may not feed thousands, but you could take time with one person at a time at the direction of the Holy Spirit. Regardless of your age bracket. God doesn't care anything about your age bracket. It's not a qualifier or a disqualifier.

"But love ye your enemies, and do good, and lend, hoping for nothing again; and your reward shall be great, and ye shall be the children of the Highest: for he is kind unto the unthankful and to the evil. Be ye therefore merciful, as your Father also is merciful."
(Luke 6:35-36)

When Jesus said be merciful the way your Father is merciful, he was saying that as a born-again creation, you have that characteristic of mercy within you. You may have buried it under some other things, but you have the DNA of your Father God. When a kind and thoughtful woman has been hurt--very badly or repeatedly--she will hide her kindness and thoughtfulness in the future thinking that these attributes made her an open target for abusers. She will develop a hard outer shell so that she doesn't have to experience that type of pain again. And do you want to know a secret? It's not just women who get hurt in life. Men get hurt, too, and they begin to hide their hearts so that they don't experience that type of pain again.

Many of us have our shields up or hide our struggles, but Jesus came to heal the broken-hearted and to bind up those wounds if we will receive the healing He offers. We know negative things are going to happen in ministry and in service to God, but we have a Comforter. It's the Holy Ghost. He is our Comforter, Counselor, Helper, Intercessor, Advocate, Strengthener and Standby. He is the only shield we need. So, let's allow compassion to rise up in us again because we need to develop the art of waiting on God.

How To Still the Avenger

One of the ways we've fallen short is in not proactively shutting down the voice of the enemy. Of course, the only power he has is what we've relinquished to him. When we start out ministering to others, at some point, satan will step in to discourage us from going any further by biting our hand and shutting us down. He wants to have the last word, and fear is his tactic. Once he silences us, we return to regular life.

"Out of the mouth of babes and sucklings hast thou ordained strength because of thine enemies, that thou mightest still the enemy and the avenger."
(Psalm 8:2)

This verse tells us that we have an enemy, but when we begin to praise God in the face of any snapping turtle situation that he devises, we can shut him down. It says we shut him down by praising God and in doing so, we still the enemy and the avenger. We make that enemy incapable of further movement and damage. You put an end to his devices by praise, but many of us are so intimidated that we haven't learned how to fight back. We don't know what our weapons are in the spirit realm. God's enemy is taking territory because we refuse to arrest him.

When we experience a loss in battle, if we fail to address it, it will negatively affect our faith. Face it. You read the Word, you see God's promise about a situation you're dealing with, and you put your faith out there to see that promise come to pass. When you don't experience victory, it causes you to draw back. You feel like you missed something. So let's do a case study of Abraham.

1. The Lord told Abraham to leave his family and the country where he lived. The man was 75 years old, but he obeyed.

2. After Abraham obeyed God and began on his journey, God made a promise to him saying "Unto your seed will I give this land." (Genesis 12:7)

3. By the thirteenth chapter of Genesis, we see that God had made Abraham a very wealthy man. But in Genesis fifteen, Abraham asked what God would give him since he was childless. It was at this point that God made it clear to him that he would have a child of his own, that he would be a progenitor—a parent.

4. Sarah, Abraham's wife, was weary about the whole situation and convinced Abraham to sleep with her handmaid Hagar in order to have a child. All this really did was to prove that Abraham still had pipe game and that Sarah's reproductive system was the issue because the maid did what Sarah could not do. She produced a son for Abraham.

5. Abraham had three visitors from heaven, and he showed them hospitality while they sat together under the shade of a tree near his tent door. Sarah laughed when she heard one of the visitors say she would bear a child this time next year. She laughed because she was old and because she no longer had a menstrual cycle. Even if she didn't have the reproductive problem, age was now a limiting factor.

6. Abraham was one hundred years old when Sarah bore Isaac his son.

So, how did Abraham maintain faith in the promise God had given him? We find that in Romans.

"And being not weak in faith, he considered not his own body now dead, when he was about an hundred years old, neither yet the deadness of Sarah's womb. He staggered not at the promise of God through unbelief; but was strong in faith, giving glory to God. And being fully persuaded that, what he had promised, he was able also to perform."
(Romans 4:19-21)

Here are some of Abraham's faith keys.

1. He gave no consideration to his dead body or his wife's dead body. (He may have thought "My body is dead; your body is dead, so it's impossible. Regardless of that, I refuse to look at the negatives because God is greater.)

2. He chose not to stagger about what God had promised because to stagger means to get into unbelief. (Going back and forth means your faith is weak.)

3. His faith became strong because he practiced giving glory to God. (Praise offered to the One who is incapable of failure and who is madly in love with us boosts your faith to a place of strength.)

4. He chose to be fully persuaded that God could do what He said He would do. (Being fully persuaded is a choice. Believing God is ALWAYS a choice!)

Likewise, we need to stop giving consideration to dead situations that speak the opposite of what God has promised. We enter into strong faith when we give glory to God through praise. There is something supernatural that happens when we take time to praise God. When we praise Him that his Word is true. When we tell Him that nothing is impossible with Him. When we give Him joy filled praise because we know there's no power shortage with God. When we refuse to stagger or to reel from side to side, God takes notice and He gets involved, bringing that thing to pass on our behalf. It's not natural. It's supernatural, and that's what we're called to operate in—the supernatural.

Becoming Skillful

In the introduction of this book, I talked about the evangelist who began to sing to the Lord and how beautiful and skillful she was. It takes practice to get there. I'm not saying your worship and praise isn't accepted until it gets to a certain level. That's not true. But it's worth it to take time worshipping God so that it flows effortlessly. We become skillful by getting to know Him through the written Word. How can we worship Him without knowing who He is? Why would you call Him the one true God unless you had learned it in the Word? Why would you call Him righteous or the advocate? Why would you call Him a hiding place or the One who shows lovingkindness? Why would you call Him the deliverer or the light? How could you sing out that He is gracious and merciful and good to all? How could you call Him the First and the Last, Alpha and Omega, if you do not discover it in His Word? We discover in His Word that He is the lord of hosts, the fairest of ten thousand, the light of the world, the Redeemer and The Way whose tender mercies are over all His works because we have spent time getting to know Him in His Word. And when we become well versed in His Word, then we have the necessary tools to speak His love language.

You can tell your romantic partner how wonderful they are at being a physician. You could sing their praises about how expert they are in diagnosing illnesses and in how they treat their patients with care. But your romantic partner is not a doctor but a management consultant. You've now demonstrated that you do not know that person. Knowing someone produces a true connection, and this same principle applies to knowing God and becoming skillful at worshipping Him.

Worship is a beautiful thing, and it's not one-sided. As I shared before, I have loved making up songs and singing them to God since I was a kid. One day recently, I was singing thank you to Him for loving me with His very life and with His blood. I stopped singing because I needed to drive to the bank to do some business, but I sensed that He enjoyed the song and wanted me to continue. So, I did. After parking at the bank, I watched an elderly lady walking into the building. The way she was carrying her purse made it look like there was nothing in it. After I park, I usually go through the motions of taking my seatbelt off, putting my cell phone into my purse, gathering anything pertinent and then I exit my vehicle. That is a very short span of time. But when I exited my car, this lady was already leaving the bank. When she was directly in front of me, she stopped abruptly.

"Jesus loves you," she said. "He loves you so much!" She was emphatic with that message! Coincidence? I don't think so, baby cakes. Not in the least. I almost had an outburst of tears right there in a public place. God knows how to return the love to you. He knows what you need and when you need it. He also knows how to lift you up when you're down.

You know what? I should've looked back to see if she really got into a car, or if I had had an encounter with an angel. But I was too busy fixing my face after that.

When we worship, He not only listens, but He speaks into our lives. Are we willing and ready to worship? God is dealing with the Church in this hour. He wants transformation because He's looking for production. We must turn from the lust of the eyes, the lust of the flesh, the pride of life, celebrity culture and idol worship. We give social media way too much time and end up getting snared by the algorithm. In contrast, when we refocus our efforts and begin to spend time with Him, we get overshadowed and loved by the Abba-rithm.

A Praise Testimony

God has never allowed me to be a popular person. In fact, I am an introvert. So, whenever I invited people to my home, I was not surprised when only one or two actually showed up. One year, I felt the Spirit of God nudging me to invite people over. The idea He gave me was to have a praise party. I used every excuse in my arsenal to make myself believe that no one would come. That way, I could justify not planning anything. Finally, I admitted it was the Holy Spirit and I couldn't disobey.

This was during a time in my life when one of my job responsibilities was to represent my employer at benefit fairs. I would have a table set up and employees would stop by, pick up a freebie or ask questions about their benefits. There were always numerous other vendors at the event. Benefit fairs were always interesting. There was a chiropractor at this particular fair, so when the crowd of employees died down, I approached the chiropractor, and he examined me. He confirmed what I had observed. One of my legs was shorter than the other. I decided to make an appointment to see what could be done about it.

I extended invitations to about seven ladies from my church to come to my praise party. I didn't really know how to conduct such a party, but the praise part was obvious. Right? To my surprise, they all showed up. So, we praised God for the space of an hour. Then we sat down in silence. I thought the Spirit of God would speak a word of prophecy maybe. After a couple of minutes, all eyes in the room turned to me, the host of the meeting. They began to look at my knees. One was obviously growing out. They were surprised and delighted, but I was freaking out because I could both see it and feel it.

It rouses the Father when He hears praise coming from His children on earth. He wants to do a new thing. I would suggest you have a praise party every now and then. Praise with regularity, with frequency, whether you do it with a group or on your own.

CHAPTER 7
FROM BOOT CAMP TO THE FRONTLINES

Hearing His Voice

When my daughter was a teen, she excitedly asked if she could go on a day trip with my sister and her husband and sons and her grandmother to Ohio for a barbecue festival. I said yes, and they all got into his van and left for Ohio. This was in the days when not everyone and their Maltipoo pup had a cell phone. This was in the days when if you crossed state lines, you were out of your service area. They had been gone for several hours. I was in my room reading a book (as always), learning as much as I could about the things of God. The book was very good. And then my landline phone rang.

The call came from a local funeral home in our neighborhood. I had driven past it many times. The professional man who asked to speak with me by name was very compassionate and considerate of my feelings. He began to offer me condolences as he sought to verify that I had a daughter—and he called her by name—and asked if we lived at a certain address. I verified everything he inquired about, and after expressing even more condolences, he asked if I would give him permission to go to a certain highway to retrieve her body as she had been killed in an auto accident. I shot up from my reclining position. My heart was beating violently. This was my only child! She couldn't be replaced. I've heard stories of people who lost their minds, suddenly. They snapped and lost their faculties. Because of this incident, I know how that feels. I know because I began to sense the darkness flooding into my mind. I felt myself going into a black, black place of no return and I was alone in that place. I also felt that I would not return if I were swallowed up by the grief. But before my mind snapped and my faculties shut down, I heard His voice.

"She's fine."

I found strength from somewhere and told the funeral director that he must have the wrong number, but he asked my name again, my address, my daughter's name, and he began to apologize profusely, promising to double check his facts and call back. When he called back, I was still so nervous, the blood was pulsating rapidly through my body. I was unable to do anything. He apologized but he believed his information to be accurate. That's when I heard the voice of the Holy Spirit, and he was angry then. I heard him clearly and knew He was upset when He spoke this time.

"Just go back to doing what you were doing! She is fine!" It was authoritative. I had been taught some things about the Holy Spirit, but I hadn't known that He could be strongly upset. The teaching I knew was "The Holy Spirit is a gentleman," but I felt the heat of His words that day, and I have to mention that I was glad that He wasn't upset with me.

At that point, I had a choice to make. Do I believe the funeral home, or do I believe the Holy Ghost? I knew His voice. It was clear, and He was quite upset that someone had gone to great lengths to play a gutless, mean-hearted trick on me. I had never experienced God being that upset or using that tone of voice to express how displeased He was. Strangely, I began to reassure the funeral home director that his information was false, that I had just heard the Holy Spirit tell me that my daughter, my only child, was fine and that he didn't need to worry about his reputation--which he was. He assured me that he would never make a false call to someone concerning a death that had never happened, and we ended the call. After I hung up the phone, I knew I had to follow the instructions I'd been given if I wanted to stay in faith and maintain my peace. "Just go back to doing what you were doing," He had said.

I couldn't verify that she was fine. My two choices were either become hysterical or believe I had heard the voice of God. My blood had never rushed so hard in all my life. It felt like I would explode from the pressure. But I re-opened my book, reading each word two and three times before I was able to comprehend anything that was written.

I could have snapped that day if I had not been able to hear the voice of God. Hours later, my beautiful child walked back into that house, and I embraced her like I never had before. And darkness lost again.

Folks, we can hear the voice of God in our spirit, yet there is a debate in the Church today that we cannot hear God speak to us. In the Bible, we have general instructions and an understanding of God's character, but what do we do when we need very specific instructions like I did when I was told that my only child had been killed in an auto accident on the highway? In 1 Samuel, chapter 3, we see Samuel as a young prophet in training. It was bedtime and the man he served, Eli, had gone to bed when Samuel heard his name called. He assumed it was the old man Eli calling him for something he needed, but Eli told the boy he had not called him. This happened three times before Eli told Samuel how to respond if he heard the voice again. He instructed him to say "Speak, Lord, for thy servant heareth." We must learn how to hear God's voice, and we need to know how to respond. This ability is critical for the hour we live in and for hearing how to minister to those around us.

Mary the mother of Jesus responded well when God sent an angel to talk with her. Yes, she was confused and disturbed initially when the angel began talking to her, and she had a question about how this would happen. Asking God a how question is not necessarily a sign of doubt. It can be a question about how to cooperate with what God wants to do, and that's what Mary wanted to do--cooperate with God.

"Then said Mary unto the angel, How shall this be, seeing I know not a man?"
(Luke 1:34)

"And Mary said, Behold the handmaid of the Lord; be it unto me according to thy word."
(Luke 1:38)

When all was said and done, Mary heard and responded well. This is part of the art of waiting on God.

We can hear from God, and we must respond. We cannot be on the frontlines of battle with an untrained spiritual ear that cannot hear His voice. It is imperative that we be able to hear His instructions, His answers, His strategy and even His

70

declarations of love for us. He will speak to us in critical times as well as in times He wants to bless us. At one point in my work life, the workload was increasing rapidly and the internal processes we had to follow were becoming more complicated, demanding more of our time. The emails turned into overlords that consumed our lives. I began to resent every email that populated my laptop, especially the ones that held no value. One particular email that kept appearing over the months had to do with company stock. I felt overworked and underpaid, and I was resentful about another email on purchasing company stock. As the weeks went by, each time the stock email popped up, I would open it, read the opening line and delete it for time's sake. However, one day, I slowed down because I know one of the primary ways God leads me. He shows me things. I used to joke about being God's little pet and how He would sometimes show me things like these massive angels that used to sit on top of a certain church in the neighborhood. Or an evil spirit looking at me from a man's eyes who had proposed to a young lady I was becoming friends with. His mission was to keep her involved in a false religion because she had begun to watch my life and became curious about Christianity.

I hadn't been taught about seeing in the spirit, but my eye kept being forced to look at the title of this reoccurring email. Finally, I gave in and decided I would read the whole thing. It was not what I originally thought. The email reminded me that I was already the owner of stock options and if I did not inform the company of what I wanted to do with the options, I would lose it. By the time I read the email, I was just a few days away from the deadline. I had to scramble. If I had not paid attention to the leading of the Holy Spirit, I would have lost a few thousand dollars.

We will not serve God well in 2025 and beyond if we cannot hear Him speak to us. If you haven't cultivated the ability to hear God's voice, please go back to the learning environment and search the scriptures until you develop your ability to hear from Him instead of remaining in a stubborn stance where you insist on being the weakest link in the Army of the Lord. There are many good teachers in the Body of Christ today.

Fasting

I have talked about the importance of knowing God's Word, but it is also important to fast at times, as the Spirit of God leads you. Fasting cuts through the brush of not being able to hear from God. It has other purposes, too, listed in the fifty-eighth chapter of Isaiah. Four purposes are listed there:

1. Loose the bands of wickedness
2. Undo the heavy burdens
3. Let the oppressed go free
4. Break every yoke

When you read these four purposes of fasting, think of people you can fast and pray for. There are also some promises listed that come from fasting. Your light shall break forth as the morning. Your health shall spring forth speedily. Righteousness shall go before thee. The glory of the Lord shall be your rearguard.

The New Living Translation says it like this:

"Then your salvation will come like the dawn, and your wounds will quickly heal. Your godliness will lead you

forward, and the glory of the Lord will
protect you from behind.
(Isaiah 58:8 NLT)

I don't know about you, but I need my salvation and help to break forth like the dawn. I need healing from time to time. I need my right-standing with God to be in full force and to go before me, and I sure wouldn't mind the glory of the Lord being my rear guard. Run up on that, devil 'cause I got backup!

Book of Acts

If you are still reading, it must be because you're like me. Ready for some action! Back in 2020 when family members and I piled into that hospital conference room and prayed for my son-in-law's release from death, we were determined and confident that God would grant our request. Sometime afterwards, the young man who was shot, Lamar, said this on a Facebook post. "If I was the devil, I wouldn't mess with Laverne (his sister) or Delilah" because of the way we had prayed that night. I laughed out loud. That was rib-cracking funny to me. I didn't just talk to God that night. As far as I was concerned, I was the prosecuting attorney staring down The Accuser in the courtroom and the blood of Jesus on the mercy seat in heaven was my stamp of approval. I remember saying to the devil, "You don't tell me! I tell you! Who do you think you are?"

This was a shootout at the OK Corral because of the fact that Jesus had already made an open show of Satan's defeat in the bowels of hell. Have you ever had anyone go to the trouble of coming to your house and beating the living daylights out of you on your own property? Can we say humiliating, boys and girls? I was loaded for bear, shooting everything that moved! Click, up, boom!

I'm not bragging. God did the work. Don't you want to be known for being a good servant in the house of God? God has a menu of things He would like to see get done. Don't you want Him to order off the menu and hand you an assignment? He only hands out assignments the He knows we can do. Do you want to sit around and complain and vegetate? Or do you want to be a servant in the house where there's some action going on? Even those in the secular world are looking for that explosive thing that changes the atmosphere with a burst of power, but many Christians have become so complacent that they refuse to enter the battleground. Their lives are marked by self-satisfaction to the point where they are oblivious of the danger the lost man or woman is in. Most are so self-satisfied that they are unaware of their own spiritual deficiencies, but deficiencies will get you if you don't watch out.

All Walks of Life

In the Book of Acts, people from all walks of life were involved in the work of God. On one occasion, Paul preached so long that he preached until midnight. In that house where he preached, there was a young man sitting up in the third loft named Eutychus who was trying to stay awake long enough to hear the Word of the Lord. He fell asleep and accidentally fell down three floors and died. Paul went down to him, embraced the young man and he was raised from the dead. Eutychus was just a regular fella.

There were elders in the church of Ephesus who were doing their best to hold the church together. They heard Paul's warning that wolves would come not sparing the flock of God because wolves have their own purposes which don't line up with the purposes of God. They cried when Paul left, knowing they'd never see him again. The elders were regular people who had stepped up to lead.

When Paul went to Caesarea, he stayed with Philip the evangelist, who had four daughters who were virgins, and they had the gift of prophecy. They were regular Middle Eastern girls who lived in an environment where women were expected to be quiet and unheard. But they were operating in their God-given gifts. Regular, ordinary young women.

There was another man from Judea whose name was Agabus. He was a prophet. A regular guy.

There was an older man from Cyprus whose name was Mnason who invited them to stay at his home. When he reached Jerusalem, the elders there got to Paul as quickly as they could and warned him of the existing political climate and what the people would try to do to him. Regular people—working together in the Body of Christ in the same way your blood, your veins, your heart, your muscles and your bones all work together and not against each other. When your internal organs begin to work against each other, it's called dis-ease. We have a lot of disease in the Body of Christ today, one Christian working against another. It's shameful and a disgrace to the Father.

These and many others were regular people in their everyday walk of life, doing what needed to be done for The Kingdom of God. I'm telling you it beats sitting at home watching professional newscasters spitting out false and misleading information about what's going on in the world when you could be doing your part by executing the assignments God has given you. When He orders off His divine menu, do what He asks you to do. Pray for someone. Pray with someone. Explain a scripture. Lead someone to Christ. Let the gifts operate through you. Be a giver. Volunteer at church. Mow the neighbor's lawn. Feed someone who's hungry. Help someone have fun when they're down. Be where He tells you to be. Pray, fast, live according to His Word, listen for His voice and EXECUTE YOUR ASSIGNMENT.

The Prodigal

I know we've talked about compassion, but can we hit it one more time by taking a look at the story of the prodigal son? Let's look at it from a different perspective than we did before. Here's my view of the story recorded in Luke the fifteenth chapter.

We know that multiple children can be born of the same parents, live in the same house, be raised under the same principles and beliefs of those parents, yet one may come away with a different set of values and beliefs than they were taught. The younger son had an agenda that was not based on the things his father had taught him. Something propelled him to give in to the lust of the eyes, the lust of the flesh and the pride of life. This is why he wanted his inheritance. He wanted to explore "the high life."

The painful lesson the prodigal son learned was that when the money runs out, the fun runs out. He discovered that real friends are not found in the bars and the strip joints. And all some women want is your money. These were lessons learned the hard way, but later on when he re-examined the character of his father, he discovered another important characteristic. In his heart, he knew his father would receive him back if he repented. So, his plan was to ask his father to take him back as one of his hired servants. While competing with pigs for food, he had a heavy revvy, a sudden epiphany that his father valued the servants! His heart had changed, and he was now willing to serve. But let's take a look at the older son.

"Now his elder son was in the field: and as he came and drew nigh to the house, he heard musick and dancing. And he called one of the servants and asked what these things meant."
(Luke 15:25-26)

The older son was a workaholic. He used work to try to prove his worth to his father. Music and dancing were not things he was familiar with. It was foreign to him.

The older brother had an angry response to a party being thrown for the prodigal. In verse 28, he refused to participate in this party. When his father came to speak with him, he saw that his son was angry, but his father didn't respond in kind. Scripture says he entreated his son. To entreat means to plead with, especially in order to persuade. He spoke with the older son in a persuasive manner. This man was gracious in the way Psalm 145 talks about how God is gracious.

"The Lord is gracious, and full of compassion; slow to anger, and of great mercy."
(Psalm 145:8)

The older son argued his case with his dad telling him he had worked for him for many years and had never gone against his commandments and at no time did his dad prepare a huge party for him and his friends. His accusations went on. He used this opportunity to point out that his brother had been out engaging with prostitutes and had spent all his money. How did he know his brother had been at the hoe down? Did he send out spies to investigate what the younger brother was doing? He was enraged that his father was throwing a grand party for his brother, the trespasser. His father's response was to point out that "You are always with me, and everything I have is yours."

The concept of grace and forgiveness went right over the older son's head like a zoom rocket because he was comfortable with works and not with grace. He thought he could earn a blessing when everything already belonged to him. He wanted validation of his own methods so badly that he couldn't see his father's heart for what it really was. He never opened his mouth to communicate or to ask in faith with an expectation to receive. He didn't try to accept grace.

Everything I have is yours. Can you hear that?

The reason I see this as a picture of the Church is because half of the Church has left the House to go live like the world, and the other half is sitting smugly with religious finger pointing. Parts of the church are only concerned about their own well-being and how they can get along in life without having too deep of a relationship with God. They've been lured by what the world has to offer. Status and material things are very important to them, and they'll achieve status by their own efforts if they have to. When the movement of teaching of the Word began several decades ago, people began to flock to it, and they learned that faith really is the substance of things hoped for and the evidence of things not seen. They began to know more about God and about how to use their faith for practical life answers.

With all that said, only a small sector of Christianity is proactively winning the lost. Everyone else is doing church as usual. Why? Could it have something to do with maintaining their "hell insurance?" Meanwhile, the Great Commission has been choked.

But I tell you that there is Remnant! They haven't allowed a spirit of competition to dominate their thoughts. They will not let denominationalism alter their focus. They have refused to give in to cessationists. They believe the whole Bible. Nothing will stop them from getting close to God. They are determined to serve the Father. It's in their hearts, and they won't let go. They will do great exploits as God leads them. They will get an understanding about the fires of hell, which will push them into greater compassion. They will bring in the lost, and they will make an impact in this generation.

Compassion means to stand in the gap. We stand in the gap because this is a showdown between light and darkness, and this is a Kingdom and not a religion.

Proactive Sons of Thunder

"And when they found them not, they drew Jason and certain brethren unto the rulers of the city, crying, These that have turned the world upside down are come hither also."
(Acts 17:6)

Turning something upside down upsets the ruling class. It shakes things up. Likewise, when you begin operating in spiritual things, satan fears loss and begins to fight back. Do not lapse into fear. Keep doing the works God has assigned you to do.

> "For this purpose the Son of God was manifested, that he might destroy the works of the devil."
> (I John 3:8)

This is what the reborn Christian man or woman is designed to do. It's our assignment and our purpose whether we're parents, social workers, firemen, wait staff, doctors, engineers, salespeople, entertainers, administrative people, entrepreneurs, auto repair persons or preachers. Each one of us has assignments. This is not the comparison show. There are no big you's and little me's. What God gives you to do, you can accomplish. It may be as simple as giving someone a hug or keeping a neighbor's children during an emergency. Or forgiving someone who hurt you. Forgiveness can turn another person's world upside down because they knew they were wrong and fully expected a backlash for what they did. Yet, they were given forgiveness instead of backlash. Turning the world upside down could be a prayer assignment that God hands you when everyone else is running their mouths and saying how bad things are.

Turning the world upside down could be like what Lamar said. "If I was the devil, I wouldn't mess with Laverne or Delilah." People who pray can turn some things. But turning the world upside down could also be clothing and feeding people who need it. Or having a small group meeting at your home once a month for people who haven't been able to make themselves walk into a church. It could be hugging people who are too proud to ask for a hug. Hugs break barriers!

Cameras and the entertainment industry have made life's tragedies into events that we sit and watch while munching on snacks. Where are the first responders in The Kingdom of God?

The Fruit of the Spirit

The fruit of the spirit are listed in Galatians the fifth chapter.

"But the fruit of the Spirit is love, joy, peace, longsuffering, gentleness, goodness, faith, meekness, temperance: against such there is no law."
(Galatians 5:22-23)

These nine fruit are inside of you when you are born again. They need to be developed by giving expression to them. We can also suppress them and revert to our old nature, but as we renew our minds to the Word, transformation takes place. The fruit of the spirit are spiritual forces. We need to learn how to operate in love, joy and peace. We can give longsuffering, gentleness and goodness as gifts to others. Operating in faith, meekness and temperance is powerful.

A force is active power. One example of this is the force of nature. A force has strength and energy and can be the cause of motion or change. These fruit of the spirit can cause motion and change in you as well as in others.

Imagine operating in love instead of hate. Love leaves the door open for someone to come back to you causing unity. Or it can make them curious about God.

Being joyful instead of depressed causes strength to fill you. It is a spiritual force that lifts the inner man.

The opposite of peace is turmoil, irritation and conflict. Nothing good comes from irritation and conflict, but the respect that peace produces is wonderful.

Longsuffering (or patience) is a force that encourages people. How many people abandoned their own personal development because patience was not shown to them and they were made to feel like a "less than" sign? The force of patience brings comfort and a willingness to keep making progress.

Gentleness creates an atmosphere of acceptance. The opposite of gentleness is harshness, sternness or violence, but this spiritual force can create room for love and peace to flow.

The spiritual force of goodness has to do with character, honesty and integrity. The opposite of goodness is evil, immorality and wickedness. The force of goodness has the ability to displace its opposite.

Faith is conviction of the truth, and it is a force in the spirit realm. When we hold to our faith in what God said, refusing to back down, it also creates a faithfulness toward God and His agenda.

Meekness is when you refuse to be violent, and because you do not embrace violence, it produces a strength in you that is akin to humility and submission. Submission means to get under the mission of another.

Temperance is moderation and self-restraint. When someone cannot or does not use moderation and self-restraint, some facet of their life is out of control. It is similar to when a wild animal is not yoked or restrained. That wild animal will cause havoc or destruction to anything in its path. The spiritual force of temperance leads us in the opposite direction of destruction so that we discover how to be constructive and creative.

As we develop in these fruit of the spirit, the force of them changes atmospheres and hearts.

CHAPTER 8
CHARACTER DEVELOPMENT THAT LEADS TO EXCELLENCE

A Heads Up About Pruning

The dictionary defines pruning as the selective removal of branches, stems or leaves from a plant in order to improve its health, shape or value. It can be a combination of art and science, involving knowing when and how to prune, as well as how to make proper cuts. Does this not sound like God to you?

"I am the true vine, and my Father is the husbandman. Every branch in me that beareth not fruit he taketh away: and every branch that beareth fruit, he purgeth it, that it
may bring forth more fruit."
(John 15:1-2)

God is the husbandman, the farmer. Jesus is the vine, and we are the branches that grow out of that vine. The branches give the vine opportunity to express itself. They also bear the fruit that the vine produces. The vine nourishes the branches, but the branches must produce the fruit.

1. We grow when we stay connected to Jesus.
2. We are the hands, feet and voice of Jesus in the earth expressing His love to mankind.
3. Led by the Holy Spirit, we help hurting people and bring souls into the family of God.

"Abide in me, and I in you. As the branch cannot bear fruit of itself, except it abide in the vine; no more can ye, except ye abide in me. I am the vine, ye are the branches: He that abideth in me, and I in him, the same bringeth forth much fruit: for without me ye can do nothing. If a man abide not in me, he is cast forth as a branch, and is withered; and men gather them, and cast them into the fire, and they are burned."
(John 15:4-6)

God is mission minded. He is after the precious fruit of the earth, and He's depending on us to be expressions of His love so that fruit is brought forth in the earth. Imagine a man who owns a manufacturing plant hiring workers and compensating them, but they never produce anything! That man would be miffed with both the workers and the unproductive state of his business. It would be considered a huge, embarrassing failure. Onlookers would think the man possessed no knowledge of how to run a business, but in the case of Christianity, God does know how to run His business. God prunes. Again, pruning is the selective removal of branches, stems or leaves from a plant in order to improve its health, shape and value.

God allows things to happen that amount to trims, deep cuts and removal of things in our lives that have made us comfortable enough to ignore the fact that we've been called into The Service of The King. When your life doesn't go the way you thought or planned, it is a test of whether you will continue to love, honor and follow God. Many have turned their backs on Him when life became difficult. Pruning season hurts, but we must get our focus back.

At the writing of this book, I am currently in a difficult pruning season. I was an employee of an established company for over 21 years, earning a high wage and I was a homeowner. I was in the sixteenth year of paying the mortgage on my home when I was let go from that job. I was able to pay my bills for another five or so months before I no longer had sufficient income to sustain my needs. Then the pandemic hit. I went through the foreclosure process and had to leave my home, a place where I had peace. A place where I could worship and pray for myself and others as much as I chose. I would dance before the Lord in the hallway. I loved studying the Word of God in my spare time. I had developed the discipline to pray for an hour a day before leaving my house. When on business trips, I would arise as early as I had to in order to get my prayer time in before early morning business meetings. I lived a celibate lifestyle because I didn't want to hurt the heart of God and also because I wanted to please Him. That was my heart posture, companionship or no companionship. For the last four and a half years, I have been sleeping on a sofa in my parents' house with no privacy, helping my sister tend to aging parents and driving a small car that I wonder how much longer it will last. I have felt stuck for a long time, and yes, I have wondered how this could possibly be the reward for living a holy and obedient lifestyle. But I've discovered that an obedient and holy lifestyle is baseline, a minimum starting point. It is what God expects out of all His children. It's not a place where rewards are given. God is not only looking for production. He expects it, and this is a major key that we cannot overlook.

This pruning season has been not only a test of whether or not I would continue being devoted to God, but it has changed who I am. I've put shyness under my feet. I am proactive about what God has assigned me to do, and nothing will hinder me from doing the will of God in my life. I will do what God requests of me whether anyone goes on the journey with me or not. I know on the inside that I will see turnaround and restoration soon. I've discovered the truth of Matthew 16.

"Then said Jesus unto his disciples, If any man will come after me, let him deny himself, and take up his cross, and follow me. For whosoever will save his life shall lose it: and whosoever will lose his life for my sake shall find it. For what is a man profited, if he shall gain the whole world, and lose his own soul? or what shall a man give in exchange for his soul?"
(Matthew 16:24-26)

In the American church, we've gone after Jesus to an extent, but we refuse to deny ourselves. Our comfort zones have become idols. We have not taken up His cross. We've followed Him for a few steps, then we've sat down underneath a tree in the shade. God desires fruit. He desires those who will go the distance regardless of what it costs them. He desires those who will worship Him to the exclusion of all else. I remind you that the Hebrew word for worship is the same as the word for work. Worship and work go hand in hand like lovers in a relationship. If you are attempting to be a Christ follower without working for Him, then the model is broken. Something has yet to be understood. When we worship in spirit and in truth, we gravitate towards doing works of service that please Him.

"And thou shalt love the Lord thy God with all thy heart, and with all thy soul, and with all thy mind, and with all thy strength: this is the first commandment."
(Mark 12:30)

The worship and work concept is something you are already familiar with. When someone does something good for you, you then have a desire to respond in kind and do something good for them. This is why it is critical that our minds be renewed. Then we begin thinking more like God thinks.

"For my thoughts are not your thoughts, neither are your ways my ways, saith the Lord. For as the heavens are higher than the earth, so are my ways higher than your ways, and my thoughts than your thoughts."
(Isaiah 55:8-9)

It's not time to think about heaven, dear ones. It's time to think about the harvest.

It's time to be in the God assigned place doing the God assigned thing. This doesn't mean that you run out and start doing strange things that were never assigned to you. Always remember that God is the coach, and He puts you into the game. He tells you what position to play. You don't just jump in when and where you want to. That's not how this works! We already have too many people who are preachers who should have been attorneys, accountants, janitors or office managers. There are women who have married men for their money when they should have been leading a social effort in the local community before God led them to the right man for them. There is a plethora of men who are incarcerated because fear bonded them to the ease of a criminal lifestyle versus having the courage to enter The Service of the King.

If you have given your life to Christ, learn the Word of God, learn how to pray, learn how to lead someone to Christ and become disciplined in your devotion to His purposes. These things are baseline, but we must be predisposed to service. Determined to serve even in the face of difficulties. When you are predisposed to something, it means you are more liable or inclined to a specified attitude, action or condition. Lack of exercise will predispose you to certain behaviors like laziness, excuses for not meeting goals and lack of feeling or emotion. When you begin to exercise yourself in the things of God, you will become predisposed to serve Him. And it helps to be in a company of believers whose hearts beat with love for God. Then serving Him becomes The New Normal.

Pruning occurs before God places you into a new position. It is similar to beginning a new job that starts with the orientation process.

1. Orientation

You learn company policies and what the benefits are. You learn things about the Founder and CEO of the company, as well as the company's Vision, Mission and Values.

2. Training

You are taught what the goals are for your position and how to achieve those goals. You learn what equipment to use and who your partners are.

3. Evaluation

The employee is examined for their contribution to the company and assessed for the need for additional training. They are also evaluated for possible promotion to a higher-level position.

You see, we think managers and consultants in the business world have come up with these principles, but they come from God. He takes us through orientation, training and development as well as evaluation for His purposes. He is not willing that anyone should be lost. That's His driving force. If you feel like you don't hear from God or that you don't hear from Him the way you used to, tap into what He's doing. Ask Him what He wants done and how you can help. It will be like total wax removal from your spiritual ears.

Joseph's Prison Experience

One of the greatest stories of character development is found in the Biblical story of Joseph. It's popular today to say, "Trust the process," but I don't like that phrase. I believe in trusting the God of the process because He watches over us as we go through things. Joseph was a trusting young dreamer who was processed by several negative events and became a man who could rule at the governmental level while bearing great pain. As we examine his character development, let's go through the timeline of his life from age seventeen.

"And when his brethren saw that their father loved him more than all his brethren, they hated him, and could not speak peaceably unto him."
(Genesis 37:4)

When people cannot say a kind word to you, you need to stop and examine why. If you cannot find out the origin of their behavior, why they are standoffish, there are steps you need to take in order to protect yourself because it will likely end up biting you in the end. Joseph, in his naivete, did not do this. In fact, when he had his first dream, he ran to his brothers and shared the dream with them. Dreams are very personal but can also be very exciting. It may have been his excitement that made him rush to share the dream with people who couldn't say anything nice to him. I mean, after all, they were family, and you get used to the behavior patterns of family members. When you live with someone, you identify their idiosyncrasies and cranky behaviors. Perhaps this is why he shared such a personal dream with them. But we see in verse five what their heart motivation was.

"And Joseph dreamed a dream, and he told it his brethren:
and they hated him yet the more."
(Genesis 37:5)

Multiplied hatred, born of jealousy. It was family, those he lived and walked with daily who would look for and find a way to betray him. Oh, the dangers of familiarity. We all want to be liked and supported and have common goals, but we cannot see into the hearts of others to find out what truly lodges there.

"For it was not an enemy that reproached me; then I could
have borne it: neither was it he that hated me that did magnify
himself against me; then I would have hid myself from
him. But it was thou, a man mine equal, my guide, and mine
acquaintance. We took sweet counsel together and walked
unto the house of God in company."
(Psalm 55:12-14)

When it's Bob, a stranger from a nearby city, we don't burst out telling our dream and sharing our innermost thoughts because we don't know Bob like that. We tell close friends and family members because we think we know them. Often, we don't know them the way we think we do, so we don't see the dagger when it comes with all its freshly sharpened edges.

The first lesson is not to trust someone simply because they are in close physical proximity and we are familiar with them. Seeing someone on a regular basis does not mean you can trust them. His brothers hated him, and after he shared his dream, verse eight of Genesis 37 says they hated him even more. They went from jealousy and hatred to compounded hatred. A man or woman who has heard from God needs to be able to communicate with God about what God has revealed to him or her, hold it in his heart and only share it when God releases you to. Dear one, as we discipline ourselves to become servants of God, we need to realize that God the Father is taking us somewhere once we get trained. In the military, they call it deployment—moving people to strategic locations for specific assignments. A good rule of thumb to follow is: get in, sit down, shut up and hang on. This is character development.

Joseph's brothers conspired to kill him, but not wanting blood on their hands, they changed the plan to dropping him into a pit. Slow death instead of immediate death, I guess. In other words, they went from the most serious level of felony to a lower level of felony, but they were felons nevertheless. However, another opportunity presented itself, and they changed the plan again and decided to make some money out of the whole thing by selling him to Midianite traders. When they arrived in Egypt, the Midianite traders sold him to one of

Pharaoh's officers named Potiphar. We see here that trafficking is not new at all.

As Joseph worked, Potiphar noticed two things about Joseph. Number one, he saw that the Lord was with him, and number two, he saw that everything Joseph did, the Lord made it prosper. Joseph was born a Hebrew, raised in Hebrew culture, and he believed in the God of his fathers. He knew the culture of worship and work. So, despite his circumstances, he began to work. But the second character development lesson here is that your worship should also manifest in your service to God even if you are in a captive, less than desirable situation.

In the 39th chapter of Genesis, we see that Joseph became so good at his household management job that promotion came to him. He was promoted from house boy to overseer. One Bible translation describes Joseph as handsome and well-built. It doesn't matter if you are handsome and well-built. When you begin to come into prominence and the blessing of the Lord is on you, temptation or a test will show up because you're out of the shadows now and the spotlight is on you. You look good because the blessing of the Lord is on you. You look like a delicious snack to those who have greedy, carnal appetites. Joseph's temptation and test came in the form of sexual temptation from the boss' wife.

She was so unimportant that the Bible doesn't even mention her name. She was just another female who believed in using her femininity to get what she wanted. She knew how to pose and smile and style her hair just right. She enjoyed things being handed to her. She believed the adage "It's not hurting anybody," the same phrase many use today to justify their sin. You cannot be part of God's Remnant while embracing a lower standard in your heart. This woman was literally begging Joseph for sex on a daily basis. In the end, she turned vengeful and made up a huge lie in an effort to get revenge. The fifteenth verse of the thirty-ninth chapter says she lifted up her voice and cried foul play.

Note that when she offered herself to him, Joseph could have rationalized why and how he could get away with it. He could have easily said "I didn't ask to be a slave in this house. I know how my master spends his time, when he comes and goes. I know his habits. I know I can get away with this. Besides, it's time I had a bonus, and this is it." But he didn't do that.

"There is none greater in this house than I; neither hath he
kept back anything from me but thee, because thou art his
wife: how then can I do this great wickedness,
and sin against God?"
(Genesis 39:9)

Did you notice that he didn't call it a bad idea? He called it out for what it was—great wickedness and sin. Today, we call fornication and adultery a slip-up, an entanglement or a momentary lapse in judgment. Deception presents itself like a feather-soft designer blanket before its lies smother you in shame and disgrace.

Potiphar was a proud man, and reputation mattered a great deal. There is always someone who knows how to use weaknesses like pride and status against you. His wife was that someone. They deserved each other. Know who you are dealing with. You may have to work for someone whose values are different than your own, but don't be fooled into thinking you're in good with them.

Joseph was seventeen when he was sold into slavery. I don't know how many years he served in Potiphar's house before Potiphar realized he had someone who could be trusted as overseer of his house, but Joseph was coming into his twenties, a time when sexual arousal is typically high for males. Joseph passed this test because he honored the man he was working for, but this level of honor was secondary. The primary and highest honor he had was the honor he had for God.

The third lesson in character development is that if your heart truly loves God and His Word, it will enable you to pass tests that originate from your own strong fleshly desires. If your love for Him and His Word is not high enough, you will not pass these tests. The Word of God works. It has the power within itself to work out any and every situation.

"Submit yourselves therefore to God. Resist the devil, and he will flee from you."
(James 4:7)

We are familiar with this passage but often focus on the part where the devil flees. No, the first instruction is to submit yourself to God. That part must be done first in order to get the result. The way you submit yourself to God is by submitting to the Word of God and the government of God. When you learn, receive and believe the Word of God, it becomes an epistle written in the heart, and men can read who you really are. (See 2 Corinthians 3:2.) When the Word is written on your heart, it keeps you from sinning against God.

Thy word have I hid in mine heart, that I might
not sin against thee.
(Psalm 119:11)

If you keep sinning against God, it means there is not enough of the Word of God written on your heart, and you must return to the learning environment before you are fit for service performed with excellence.

You may experience mediocre service at the local greasy diner, but when you experience a higher level of service at a fine dining establishment, you won't be eager to return to the grungy, greasy place. It probably needs an unannounced visit by the health department anyway. When the health department comes for an inspection, they will do a write-up about the long-tailed friends they found, the Brown Brothers (roaches) that were crawling around and all the health risks that were just waiting to make people sick and possibly die.

Why am I using this analogy? It's somewhat like the job evaluation mentioned earlier. Are you doing your job well? Are you hurting the Company's reputation? Are you profitable? There are some churches that need Heaven's Health Department to do a surprise visit so that the spiritual health of the members is addressed. If you're serving in God's Kingdom, don't be a health risk to the Body of Christ, especially if you are called to a ministry office such as apostle, prophet, evangelist, pastor or teacher.

Following that non-incident, Joseph was thrown into prison. We don't read where the text says that Joseph then went into depression, anxiety or bitterness, although I'm sure he had emotions to deal with. Instead, we see that even in the prison environment, he was promoted once again.

"But the Lord was with Joseph, and shewed him mercy, and
gave him favour in the sight of the keeper of the prison. And
the keeper of the prison committed to Joseph's hand all the
prisoners that were in the prison; and whatsoever they did
there, he was the doer of it. The keeper of the prison looked
not to anything that was under his hand; because
the Lord was with him, and that which he did,
the Lord made it to prosper."
(Genesis 39:21-23)

I would say that the fourth lesson in character development is to push past depression, anxiety and bitterness because these things will hinder you from operating in the favor of God. It will keep you from operating in your gift, whatever that gift may be. Depression is a wild card that can eat up everything in your life, even your potential, but if you force yourself to keep operating in your gift and in your assignment, a shift will happen and deliverance will come.

God's remnant is comprised of those who yearn to serve God and see the supernatural take place. These believers are inextricably addicted to Jesus. Many of these remnant believers are also broken and hurting, but they serve God anyway.

In prison, Joseph was operating in his administrative gift as well as his spiritual gift (dream interpretation). In the fortieth chapter of Genesis, the king's chief butler and chief baker were thrown into prison, and the captain of the guard put them under Joseph's charge. After some time had passed, both the butler and the baker had dreams. The next morning, Joseph went in to speak with them.

"And Joseph came in unto them in the morning, and looked upon them, and, behold, they were sad. And he asked Pharaoh's officers that were with him in the ward of his lord's house, saying, Wherefore look ye so sadly to day?"
(Genesis 40:6-7)

Take note of Joseph's approach. Instead of telling them "Suck it up, buttercup. We're all in the same sad situation," he was solicitous of them. He wanted to know what was wrong and how he could help. The fifth area of character development that we see here is that Joseph was developed in meekness. He was serving while wounded, reaching out to the hurting while enduring his own life injuries. If the only time you can serve others is while things are great for you, you've found your ceiling and you won't go past it. You'll be locked into that ceiling until you decide to break through. Breakthrough to the next level happens when you serve while wounded, giving no thought to your own pain.

"Then said Jesus unto his disciples, If any man will come after me, let him deny himself, and take up his cross, and follow me. For whosoever will save his life shall lose it: and whosoever will lose his life for my sake shall find it."
(Matthew 16:24-25)

Personally, I've experienced times of exasperation when I've declared I'm not doing another thing for anybody else until somebody does something for me and stomped off. Lying lizard! I was just having a temper tantrum, but eventually, I got over it and returned my focus to how I could help someone else. When God truly has your heart, you may have a tantrum here and there, but your addiction to Him and to serving Him won't let you escape. It won't allow you to turn rogue. A rogue will go into isolation, become aberrant, dangerous and uncontrollable. But it is the love of God that constrains us (2 Corinthians 5:14).

You will cry sometimes. OK, a lot of times maybe, but those who love God more than they love themselves pull it together, and they get back at it. This is character development.

Areas of character development:

1. Keep your mouth shut and don't trust everyone. Communicate with God about His plans for you.
2. True worship of God shows up in your work.
3. A genuine love of God and His Word will enable you to pass difficult testing.
4. Forcefully and deliberately refuse depression and continue to operate in your gift.
5. Keep serving while wounded.

There are so many stories of people who birth their destiny while they are in the grips of pain. Killer pain that would stop most from serving a God that they cannot see with the natural eye. Pastor Andrew Brunson was imprisoned in Turkey in 2016 for preaching the gospel. That imprisonment almost broke him until his wife encouraged him to do two things—to worship daily and to dance before the Lord. The unfair imprisonment lasted for a couple of years, but he did worship and he did dance before the Lord, and eventually, he was released from prison. Brunson's predicament ignited a worldwide prayer movement that showed the world something significant about the power of prayer. Andrew Brunson went from pain to purpose to power.

Being in the service industry is difficult because it requires interaction with people. I observe the behaviors of people in everyday life, and sometimes, I have to filter my thoughts with the reminder that not everyone was raised by Joe and Shirley (my parents) or else they wouldn't do certain things. You may have a similar thought that keeps you from being unnecessarily judgmental. Being excellent in service to God is similar to this. We must realize that not everyone is at the same level of development in spiritual things, but Holy Spirit inspired service is still necessary. Keep in mind that it's the people you do the most for who seem to turn on you the fastest, and don't be surprised by this. It is godly character development and the supernatural love of God that will keep you serving God and serving people.

This is the art of waiting on God. Let Him develop you into the person He always intended you to be.

CHAPTER 9
A CALL TO ACTION

Why Would Anyone Want To Sign Up For Service?

This call to action requires introspection and self-examination. However, this is 2025 and this army, The Remnant of God, must move quickly and we must move now. Those trained and equipped must move to the front now. Others who are inspired to do the same will come behind us, ready to obey God. Still, I pose these questions. Why would anyone sign up for the pain and self-sacrifice of serving others when your energies could be used to build your life, your purposes, your chosen relationships, your vacations and your retirement plans? What are the incentives to being a servant?

I asked a family friend who has been in the military for decades why people sign up to go into military service. He listed five things that motivate sign-ups:

1. Travel
2. Benefits
3. Camaraderie
4. A sense of belonging to something bigger than themselves
5. Retirement

In my thoughts, the way these five things correspond to serving God are: When you hook yourself to God, He takes you places you've never been before and you get to do amazing things that you never knew were possible. God looks after His own and He sees to it that benefits flow into your life. I've shared at least one testimony in this book about how God made sure I received benefits. The fellowship and camaraderie of like-minded believers is very powerful because one soldier has the ability to strengthen another. I cannot underestimate belonging to something bigger than yourself. No matter how much I love being on the beach, I still realize that tending to our natural, personal lives leaves a great deal to be desired. The "us four and no more" mentality is not fulfilling. Selfishness always leaves a big, gaping hole, while undertaking a more noble mission has great satisfaction attached to it. Lastly, God's retirement plan is out of this world. It's the only way to go.

Here is another thought to consider. If Person A (Alan) consistently provides, and Person B (Betty) consistently receives provision without reciprocity, one of these persons is a giver and the other is a consumer. Does this type of relationship and interaction happen? Yes, but how long is it viable and satisfying? This is a hard truth I'm about to share with you, but this is the danger we fall into when we serve while wondering what we can get in return.

"But love ye your enemies, and do good, and lend, hoping for
nothing again; and your reward shall be great, and ye shall be
the children of the Highest: for he is kind unto the unthankful
and to the evil. Be ye therefore merciful, as your Father also
is merciful. Judge not, and ye shall not be judged: condemn
not, and ye shall not be condemned: forgive, and ye shall be
forgiven. Give, and it shall be given unto you; good measure,

pressed down, and shaken together, and running over, shall men give into your bosom. For with the same measure that ye mete withal it shall be measured to you again."
(Luke 6:35-38)

Loving your enemies, doing good and hoping for nothing in return, being merciful, refusing to be judgmental or condemning others—all these things are hard on the flesh and the emotions. God is not asking you to lie down and become a doormat, but if you are a servant of God, it is dangerous to fall into the mentality of horizontal reciprocity. Please be careful of this trap. This scripture in Luke 6 clearly states that it is God who rewards us. But Delilah, it says men will give in to our bosom. Yes, God is the one who motivates the heart of a person to give to you. Make sure that you don't hand pick the one who should do something for you.

Did Jesus really say that the one who serves is greatest? Yes, He did (Matthew 23:11). We've gotten it wrong by idolizing the wealthy, the celebrity, the highly paid sports figure and the multi-millionaires. Many run to gain the attention of these people thinking that they will get insider information on how to achieve the same thing. Some people chase status so hard that it's difficult not to label them as obnoxious.

"Then came to him the mother of Zebedee's children with her sons, worshipping him, and desiring a certain thing of him. And he said unto her, What wilt thou? She saith unto him, Grant that these my two sons may sit, the one on thy right hand, and the other on the left, in thy kingdom. But Jesus answered and said, Ye know not what ye ask. Are ye able to drink of the cup that I shall drink of, and to be baptized with the baptism that I am baptized with? They say

unto him, We are able. And he saith unto them, Ye shall drink indeed of my cup, and be baptized with the baptism that I am baptized with: but to sit on my right hand, and on my left, is not mine to give, but it shall be given to them for whom it is prepared of my Father."
(Matthew 20:20-23)

Wow, mom, your priorities were off. She tried to use worship for selfish motives. This is not the type of prayer request you want to put before God. You don't get this kind of reward with a simple ask. God has great respect for service, for production and for self-sacrifice. He doesn't hold in high esteem those who sit around wanting to be served and lauded for their accomplishments while they watch a world dying around them. He highly prizes the one who knows how to serve.

Favor comes on the one who serves God from the heart. Favor can get you into places and blessings that degrees and cliques cannot.

Another significant way in which the Kingdom of God is different from the world is in the area of strengths and weaknesses. In the world, if you are weak, you get trampled and taken advantage of. You get squashed like a bug if you show any weakness or even tenderness. Your guard must be up at all times. You have to be on the lookout for those who seek to take advantage of you, but weakness is not frowned on in God's Kingdom.

The Apostle Paul was having trouble with a messenger of satan that was sent to strike at his ministry with force. Paul sought the Lord three times asking Him to make it leave. Jesus answered Paul's request with this:

"And he said unto me, My grace is sufficient for thee: for my strength is made perfect in weakness. Most gladly therefore will I rather glory in my infirmities, that the power of Christ may rest upon me. Therefore I take pleasure in infirmities, in reproaches, in necessities, in persecutions, in distresses for Christ's sake: for when I am weak, then am I strong."
(2 Corinthians 12:9-10)

Why sign up for service? Because God covers you and fills in where you are weak. Not to mention the fact that in heaven, there will be notable rewards handed to those who committed themselves to a life of service.

There are other things that are valued differently in the Kingdom of God that bump up against the world's way of doing things. For instance, Jesus was constantly in conflict with the religious authorities of his day because he let them know that their long, complicated lists of rules and regulations were void of both power and love. No, he wasn't telling them to forsake the Law. He was letting them know that the letter killeth, but the spirit of it gives life. It was a matter of the heart, and their hearts were hardened. A hard heart is a closed door.

"But this shall be the covenant that I will make with the house of Israel; After those days, saith the Lord, I will put my law in their inward parts, and write it in their hearts; and will be their God, and they shall be my people."
(Jeremiah 31:33)

God's Kingdom operates differently. The things that God values are different than what the world values. Why would anyone want to serve rather than be a consumer waiting for a handout? Because there's joy in serving. It's rewarding, and it's productive. Serving in God's Kingdom is the only way to see His Kingdom come in the earth. There has been much pain in the lives of people because the servants have gone missing, and the laborers have not gone after the harvest of souls. In the past, the Church has not placed a high priority on training the everyday Christian believer on how to reach the lost or in how to disciple them. I cannot emphasize strongly enough that the time to do these things is now. Not next year, not next month. Now!

The Time for Service Is Now

If you've been taught the Word of God, it's time to reach out. If you haven't been trained, you can still keep going hard after God and the things of God by learning of him and taking his yoke upon you. You will get processed, but it's so much better to start on the journey God has for you than it is to lie dormant and unfulfilled. Why should you get to enjoy the joys of heaven one day but never tell anyone else about the love of God?

"For this purpose the Son of God was manifested, that he might destroy the works of the devil."
(1 John 3:8)

We are needed, friends, and the time for service is now. God's enemy, the devil, has destroyed many. If you listen to some of the music today, you discover how hopeless many have become. The lyrics tell all. I don't need to make an exhaustive list of the heart-wrenching situations people find themselves in. People are hurting. They are confused. They see no answers, and we stand right next to them with The Answer, afraid to share, afraid to participate in the divine encounter God wants to provide to them. Every time we have an opportunity to pour into the life of an unbeliever, more of satan's evil plans gets destroyed.

Are We Void of Compassion?

Check yourself to see if you indulge in self-righteousness. Self-righteousness is closely related to pride. I know the topic of this section is compassion, but let's see what role self-righteousness and pride have played.

> "Pride goeth before destruction, and an
> haughty spirit before a fall."
> (Proverbs 16:18)

Self-righteousness lives big in the church today. One church thinks they are better than another. They preach and teach better. They know the Word better. They dress better. They conduct church services in a more effective and powerful way, not realizing that self-righteousness has become their god more than Jehovah ever was. Religion activities do not produce anything positive for the Kingdom of God. Satan is very pleased that self-righteousness kills compassion for others in the Body of Christ. Denominations unknowingly become self-seeking factions that accomplish less and less for the glory of God. The lost are ignored, and not many go after the harvest.

I want to say this again. Self-righteousness killed compassion and this holds the message of grace captive. As a certain television character used to say, "Relax, relate, release." You cannot release anything (the Good News) if you're judging others. If you cannot relate to those who are lost just as you were once lost, you are operating in self-righteousness. Relax into the rhythm of God's grace—not the rhythm of the rules you think people should follow.

You may be agitated because I keep repeating myself, but there's a nasty, cruel backstory going on here. It's more cruel than homelessness, fornication, gang rape, murder, governmental scandals, spousal cheating, lying or anything you can think of. I'm telling you that self-righteousness has killed the Christian mission. We need to repent. Immediately! People are dying and going to hell while we indulge in infighting, malaise, and are preoccupied with carnal pursuits in our comfort zones. It ought not be like this. Don't you hear the heart of God crying out to you, asking you to take your place in service? Hell is for eternity just as heaven is for eternity.

It's not time to think about heaven. It's time to think about the harvest. Who knew that self-righteousness would kill compassion and that lack of compassion would suffocate grace? Were you at the murder scene? Probably. Did you participate in the crime? Examine yourself. This is a tragic story inside the Church today, an ugly secret. Take the blinders off because the time for service is now!

Armed for Battle With A Rear Guard

There is a prominent teacher in the Body of Christ who tells about a meeting where Christians were being taught about the authority of the believer. At some point during this service, the whole group began to say together:

Push him back, push him back

Way back, way back!

Times of fellowship with other believers cannot be substituted by anything else. Strengthening often happens when we meet together. We have a responsibility today to push the enemy back by making ourselves available to God in service. We shouldn't see it as responsibility alone because it's also opportunity. It's opportunity to go somewhere with God and to have a greater mindset and focus than the natural side of living on earth. It's an opportunity to go beyond the limitations of the natural world. One scripture that I believe will hallmark my life is found in Second Corinthians.

"Now thanks be unto God, which always causeth us to triumph in Christ, and maketh manifest the savour of his knowledge by us in every place."
(2 Corinthians 2:14)

Jesus is the One who is causing us to triumph. He causes us to win. Yes, we go through the processes of pain, loss, learning what ignorance costs, betrayal, the difficulty of interpersonal relationships and many other things, but through it all, He's there molding and shaping us if we will let Him. We're going somewhere with God, and He will use us to spread the knowledge of Christ everywhere like a sweet perfume. I'm telling you that getting to a place where you can hear from Him and then acting according to what He has said is pretty awesome. We're going somewhere with Abba. I have sat and cried when I've received a greater revelation of how much God loves and adores me. It absolutely floors me. I will tell you this. The first time you see Jesus, it won't be like you think.

The first time you see him, it will shut down every negative thing that's on the inside of you. What do I mean by that?

We all have things going on inside us that others can't see with the naked eye. Worry, depression, sadness, selfishness, doubt, lust, manipulativeness, impatience, neurotic impulses, arrogance, judgmental, cowardly, aggressive traits, narcissistic, disloyal, inflexible, rabble rouser—too many to name. When you see Jesus, all those tendencies that are churning on the inside of you will shut down as if someone suddenly hit the "off switch." None of these things can stand in His presence. When you see Jesus, you will know that you are looking at pure love. Pure Love shuts down all the noise. The brightness of His love and glory cannot be compared to anything you've ever seen or experienced. It's absolutely stunning. You will realize that we never should have developed an attachment style to these negative things because He loves us so much. These traits and tendencies don't stand up to the love of our Savior. They run and flee when we connect with Him, seeing him as he is. His presence washes us free and clear of all negativity. There is no contest.

So, you decide to give God your yes. Now what? What about the things you don't know yet? Do I need a mentor? How do I go forward? What if I make a mistake?

One Michigan winter, I woke up to a very cold morning. Ice had coated the sidewalks and streets. Snow is one thing, but ice is another because it's more dangerous to navigate than the softness of snow. I got dressed for work dreading the conditions. I walked to my car hoping against hope that the ice situation wouldn't be too bad, but from the news reports, I knew better. As soon as I got to my car, I saw a huge circle of hard ice that I wouldn't be able to step over or go around. I had to navigate it slowly and carefully. On my second step into it, my foot slipped and my body began to fall into a backward motion. I knew my head would slam into the hard sidewalk. There was no ability to recover mid-fall. As I was going down, I suddenly felt something hit me in the middle of my back and push me back up on my feet, keeping me from crashing into the cold, hard, iced cement. There was no way in the natural for me to recover from that fall, but in the supernatural, I was lifted upright and I was able to get into my car and go to work.

God has your back! Get in the car and go to work.

Don't Give a Stink Offering!

You know now that God highly values service. He loves a good waiter, but I must caution you not to bring God a stink offering. Here's what I mean. Reading the Old Testament may be difficult, even a little exhausting, but when you read the Book of Leviticus, you find out that God desired a certain type of offering. He did not want and would not accept a sickly looking animal, an animal missing a leg or one with a blemish. Animals with flaws were not acceptable. God instructed them to bring their best.

We don't bring animals for sacrifice today because Jesus was the sacrifice God gave in order to redeem us. He gave His best. Likewise, we are to give our best, not giving Him our leftovers. If we present something that did not cost us anything, it is a stench in the nostrils of God. We must practice giving God maximum effort, and we are energized to do this by first spending time in His presence. He deserves our best-in-class service. A life of serving God is the most exciting and the most rewarding life you will ever live. Being a vessel that God can use to bring the supernatural to pass creates hunger to see Him do more. It is amazing when He heals the broken-hearted, when captives are delivered and set free. Or when the blind recover their sight and the bruised are liberated when it looked like they'd be held down forever. Let's give Him our best and not our least. This is the art of waiting on God.

I must give a final reminder about the enjoyment of short-term pleasures versus pursuing meaningful goals assigned by God. It's fine to have good times in life. I would even say that fun is a necessary thing, but making short-term pleasures a priority has the ability to eliminate any motivation to follow God's plan for your life. If you are overly consumed with how much you can get out of this life on earth, please know that this has already replaced your devotion to God. Everyone else may be living their lives this way, and it may seem normal, but normal is not only overrated, it's deceitful as well. Earth is not our home. It is only a workstation where we're called to operate in the supernatural, not the natural.

> "If ye then be risen with Christ, seek those things which are above, where Christ sitteth on the right hand of God. Set your affection on things above, not on things on the earth. For ye are dead, and your life is hid with Christ in God. When Christ, who is our life, shall appear, then shall ye also appear with him in glory. Mortify therefore your members which are upon the earth; fornication, uncleanness, inordinate affection, evil concupiscence, and covetousness, which is idolatry: For which things' sake the wrath of God cometh on the children of disobedience."
> (Colossians 3:1-6)

It's not time to think about heaven. It's time to think about the harvest!

SYLLABUS OFFER

Believers strengthen each other when they fellowship and study together. A syllabus for self- and/or group study is available for purchase at www.delilahspivey.com. The syllabus is based on The Art of Waiting on God.

Please visit my Facebook author page, The Art of Waiting on God.

PRAYERS

Ephesians 1 Prayer

I pray today that the God of our Lord Jesus Christ the Father of glory would give unto me the spirit of wisdom and revelation in the knowledge of Him. I pray that the eyes of my understanding be enlightened, that I may know what is the hope of His calling and what the riches of the glory of His inheritance in the saints is. I pray to be acquainted with the exceeding greatness of His power toward us who believe, according to the working of His mighty power, which He wrought in Christ when he raised him from the dead and set him at his own right hand in the heavenly places.

Love Prayer

Lord, I endeavor to love You with all my heart, all my soul, all mind and all my strength and to love my neighbor as myself. The love of God is shed abroad in my heart by the Holy Spirit, and when You show me my assignment for this week, I will hear Your voice and I will obey. I make myself available to You.

Fasting Prayer

Father, as I go on this fast today, I pray that You loose the bands of wickedness concerning _____. Free those who are wrongly imprisoned. Undo the heavy burdens in the life of _____. Let the oppressed go free. _____ _____ is oppressed, and I command that oppression to bow down in the name of Jesus. Break every yoke. I speak to the yoke holding _____, and I command it to be broken now. Jesus came to heal the brokenhearted, to preach deliverance to the captives and recovering of sight to the blind. He came to set at liberty them that are bruised. This is my request, Father, in the name of Jesus.

(In this prayer, feel free to call out the names of persons you are praying for.)

Prayer for the Stubborn

God, Your Word says in 1 Samuel 15:23 that stubbornness is as iniquity and idolatry. Lord, I pray about the stubbornness that is bound in the heart of (_____). The heart of every person is in Your hand, Lord, and you can turn it whichever way you please. Please turn (_____) from the idolatry of self-worship and presumption. I command fear to leave now and may Your peace fill that place in their heart and mind. Loose them from the captivity of pride and that spirit of deception. I ask that You give them the peace of God that they may begin to rejoice in You and in the wisdom of God. I thank You that stubbornness has to bow down now in the name of Jesus!

The Spirit of Wisdom and Revelation

Father, I must have the spirit of wisdom and revelation of Christ and His Word. If I am to grow; if I am to minister wisdom and instruction to others, I must have the spirit of wisdom and revelation in the knowledge of Jesus. I know You have made it available to me, so I receive it by faith right now. I thank You that I am becoming more like You every day. I receive from You freely. Thank You.

Prayer for the Lost & An Opportunity to Minister to the Lost

Father, two of the greatest evangelism tools are preaching the gospel and loving people. I put love first, and in accordance with Your Word, I say that the love of God is shed abroad in my heart by the Holy Spirit. I walk with love; I see with love; I think with love. Pour out Your love today, Lord. Do it through me. There will be cries of great anguish in hell, cries of regret that cannot be answered. I know You hear the cries of lost hearts, Father, who have not passed into their eternal destination. So please use me to reach someone this day. I am available to You.

Freedom from Pornography

Father, this is the will of God, that we abstain from all sexual immorality. I ask that You loose _____ from impurity and covetousness. These things are not proper among Your children. Jesus has already set _____ free. Pull him/her out of this yoke of slavery now in Jesus' name. Loose him/her from this band of wickedness that is confining and constricting him/her in the spirit realm. I proclaim that he/she stands firm in purity and in the ways of God because he/she is loosed from bondage now. Praise you, Father.

Righteousness Faith Confession

Father, according to Second Corinthians 5:21, You made Jesus to be sin for us. He knew no sin that we might be made the righteousness of God in him. I've been made the righteousness of God in Christ Jesus. I have right-standing with God in the earth. Sin has no dominion over me. I rule, I reign and I dominate in Jesus' name!

Sinner's Prayer

Dear Heavenly Father, I come to You in the name of Jesus. You said that whoever confesses with his mouth the Lord Jesus and that God raised him from the dead would be saved. I am saying with my mouth that I believe Jesus is the Son of God. I believe He was raised from the dead. I confess Him as my Lord and Savior. Your Word says that if any man be in Christ Jesus, he is a new creature. I am a new creature and a member of the family of God right now.

About The Author

Delilah Spivey was born again and Spirit filled at the age of 13. She grew up loving church, but along the way, she began to yearn to see the move of God in everyday life. She worked in corporate America for over 40 years and graduated magna cum laude with an Associate's degree in 2013. Delilah became a member of an excellent teaching church in Southfield, Michigan for more than thirty years. While there, she served in various volunteer roles, of which two were very important to her development. One was the soul-winning team, and the other was as a small group leader, a role she held for eight years.

Soul winning and discipleship are embedded in her heart because of the importance of adding to the Body of Christ (Mark 16:15) as well as discipling the Body (Ephesians 4:16) so that it becomes mature and healthy, operating from a place of supernatural love.

Ms. Spivey has been smitten with God since her pre-teen years, and He has been smitten with her.

I would like to thank Melissa Schultz of www.melissaschultzministries.com for her every effort in supporting me as I wrote my first book. Mrs. Schultz, you are a top-notch servant and teacher in God's Kingdom!

www.ingramcontent.com/pod-product-compliance
Lightning Source LLC
Chambersburg PA
CBHW052113090426
42741CB00009B/1798